KILLERS, THIEVES, TRAMPS & SINNERS

▼

Also by Peter McGahan

Urban Sociology in Canada (second edition)
Police Images of a City
Crime & Policing in Maritime Canada

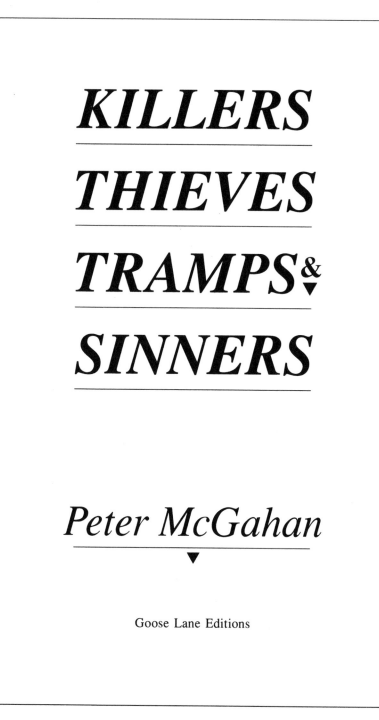

KILLERS
THIEVES
TRAMPS&
SINNERS

Peter McGahan

▼

Goose Lane Editions

Published with the assistance of the Canada Council, the New Brunswick Department of Tourism, Recreation & Heritage and the University of New Brunswick, 1989.

Book design by Julie Scriver
Printed in Canada by Wilson Printing

Photographs appear courtesy of the Moncton Museum, the Provincial Archives of New Brunswick (PANB), the Public Archives of Nova Scotia (PANS) and the Provincial Archives of Prince Edward Island (PAPEI).

Canadian Cataloguing in Publication Data

McGahan, Peter
Killers, thieves, tramps and sinners

ISBN 0-86492-114-4

1. Criminals — Maritime Provinces — History.   I. Title.

HV6809.M4M33 1989   364'.9715   C89-098657-6

Goose Lane Editions Ltd.
248 Brunswick Street,
Fredericton, New Brunswick
Canada E3B 1G9

Contents

KILLERS, THIEVES, TRAMPS & SINNERS

▼

The home of Evangeline.   (PANS)

INTRODUCTION

In August, 1890 an American tourist from Massachusetts lodged for several weeks at Wolfville's American Hotel. She had never before experienced such peace. Indeed all the communities she encountered in Nova Scotia through her travels were marked by the same character: "all are restful, and here there is no hustle, no hurry, everyone goes easily and quickly about their work or pleasure. During a fortnight's stop here I have not yet seen even a boy quicken his pace to a run, so little haste is there for anything" (*The Acadian,* 22 August 1890). No doubt other visitors of the time were similarly moved. Yet within this "Acadia of rest and peace" those who were not transient sojourners saw a greater degree of turbulence — the quest for a reliable police force, for control over disorderly youth, for victory over the liquor trade, for defense against the threats to property and person. The "world we have lost" in the Maritimes was not a peaceful world. Amidst our contemporary problems of drug use, sexual abuse, burglary, and terrorist assaults, our eyes cast back to a past era supposedly more orderly, more harmonious. As with the Massachusetts tourist, our image is certainly in part illusory.

This is evident if we take a different "tour," if we enter the world of "Killers, Thieves, Tramps and Sinners."

The selections included in this book illustrate some of the types of crimes and offences encountered in the late nineteenth-century Maritime comunities. Such places as Charlottetown, Digby, Moncton, Halifax and the Annapolis Valley were touched by the "disrespectable," by those who challenged the rule of law, by those who grasped a flawed morality, by those who could not be contained within the bounds of harmony.

I am very grateful for the support and encouragement of Peter Thomas in completing this work. I am indebted to Julie Scriver for guidance in preparing the manuscript for publication. I wish to acknowledge the invaluable assistance of the staff of the Provincial Archives in New Brunswick, Nova Scotia and Prince Edward Island and of the Moncton Museum. Wilfred Morris and Jo-Anne Stevens contributed to the photos in the chapter "Murder at Bear River." Continued contact with Dalhousie's Atlantic Institute of Criminology has been especially rewarding. The keen interest of Elizabeth McGahan in this project was of significant help.

Peter McGahan

CONFESSIONS OF A BIGAMIST

Public morality could be challenged, as the occasional case of bigamy illustrated. At his trial in September, 1879, at Dover, Maine, a Baptist preacher, Rev. Manly Carlyle Montague Steadman, was charged with this offence. He was indicted for marrying a local resident, L. Estelle Gray, while still married to Rachel M. Smith of New Brunswick. In his defense, Steadman argued that his marriage to the Smith woman had not been legal as indeed at the time he had another wife, Georgia E. Campbell, now deceased and whom he had married in 1874. The jury was not sympathetic. After little more than thirty minutes they returned with a guilty verdict. Steadman had been a resident of Moncton where the case generated considerable interest, especially in light of his double life as preacher and seducer.

My age is 27. I have resided in Nova Scotia, New Brunswick, Maine and Minneapolis, Minn. In Nova Scotia I lived in the towns of Amherst and Truro and for a short time in Halifax and in some other towns. In New Brunswick I have lived in Elgin, Parish of Salisbury, Moncton and Dundas. My father lives in Elgin, N.B. In the first part of the year 1874 I resided in my father's house in Elgin. In the early spring of 1874 I went to Moncton, N.B., then to Sackville, frequently being in Amherst and Truro. I was also in Berwick and Halifax, N.S., during a part of the time in 1874. Late in the year of 1874 was at Pollett's River, N.B., where I taught school. I taught another term in 1875. After that I remained a short time at my father's home. In the fall of 1877 I had business up the St. John River. I resided there some time; was preaching there. During January, 1878 I went to Kars, N.B., to assist Rev. Mr.

Stringer in holding revival services at that place. Was there six weeks; then went to Long Reach, Kings Co. on the St. John River and had services there. At the close of these services I was requested to remain and act in capacity of pastor of a small church in May 1878.

I was in St. John frequently during the following months and during this time was assistant pastor at Belyea Cove. I left Long Reach last of May. Went to Belyea Cove and from there in company with my wife to Tauntonville, N.S. Her maiden name was Georgia E. Campbell. Went with her to Tauntonville in June, 1878. Remained there about two weeks, then went to Moncton, N.B. Left St. John 1st or 3rd of July, 1878, in steamer "City of Richmond," to Eastport and Portland, then to Bath. Then I took a small steamboat to Georgetown, where I arrived July 3rd. Remained here for a while, making my home with my uncle, J.A. Steadman. Came to Dover in August, upon invitation of Baptist church of this place. Received a unanimous call to become their pastor. In Sept. 1878 left this place for Bath and from there to Georgetown, where I remained a few days and returned from there directly to this place, via Newport. I next saw my wife at her father's house in June. I received news of the death of my wife last of October from her father, and also from her friend Nellie G. Campbell. I believed the information to be true and still believe it. I remained at Foxcroft until May 14th, 1879, then went to Minneapolis, Minne. Remained there until June 9th. I was arrested by order of authorities of this State upon charge of bigamy on the 4th day of June and upon [the] evening of June 9th left for Maine in the company of W.E. Parsons, special officer of the State. I travelled in irons from Minnesota to Foxcroft, Me. Remained in Foxcroft 4 or 5 days and underwent an ex parte examination and was deposited in Bangor jail for safe keeping. Have remained there until brought to this place this week. I was married to Miss L. Estelle Gray of Dover, on 23rd of Feb., 1879 by Rev. H. A. Loring. I received the news of the death of my wife in Oct., 1878.

I married the daughter of J.C. Campbell of Tauntonville, N.S., in August 1874, became acquainted with her in 1873. Her maiden name was Georgia Ellen. Was known by the name of Nellie Campbell. I met her in Amherst, N.S. and Sackville, N.B. in 1873. She was then at school near Sackville, N.B. My courtship was for about a year after I first saw her. She was very much attached to me and I to her. I seduced her. She was about 17 when I married her. I got acquainted with her away from her father's house and seduced her. That fact hastened the marriage. She was a Catholic. I was Baptist, son of a Baptist clergyman. I was then residing at Moncton and Amherst, was not engaged in any particular business, was indulging in the vain pursuits of pleasure. I attended many picnics. She wished to be married by the priest; I consented to it. We went to the picnic; Mrs. Cuthbertson, my aunt, and a second cousin, John Steadman, went to the picnic with me. We met Miss Georgia E. Campbell at Dorchester, and went to the picnic together. I told my aunt that I expected to be married before I went back. We took a team and I drove to Memramcook, N.B., where we called at the residence of a Catholic clergyman named Patrick T. Goucher. I paid him $10, went to the chapel and was married before the altar, according to the Catholic form. He wished me to renounce my Baptist faith and become a Catholic. I could not do this, but agreed that our children should be educated in the Catholic faith. Mrs. Cuthbertson of Upton and John Steadman of Moncton were present. The priest gave my wife a certificate of the marriage, which certificate I left in my trunk at Minneapolis. After this we came to Moncton and lived together as husband and wife. We then went to Truro where we met the father of my wife, at Victoria Hotel, I think. He was very indignant when he found we were married. I told him I married her by her wish and my own. He roundly abused me when I told him I married from a wish to save her character. He then forbid her his house unless she abandoned me. We then considered the situation. I was twenty-two, she only seventeen. I was poor and needed all I could raise to complete my education. We decided to separate for a time, promising her father to have no correspondence. I then travelled and visited various places, writing to my wife, according to a secret arrangement, as often as four or five times a week for several weeks. I received no answers. While at Berwick I received a letter from my wife's father, saying he wished all correspondence to cease. He also stated that his daughter was very sick from a cause which I well knew. In the fall of 1874, I was at Pollett's River and wrote several letters to my wife from there and received no reply until November or December, when her father returned my letters, and a newspaper containing the news of her death. I cut the slip from that paper, which I kept until I met my wife again in 1878. I gave that slip to her then and a letter which I received from her father, that accompanied the paper when I received it. I met her in St. John in April 1878.

In the year 1874 and part in 1875 I taught school at Pollett's River and boarded part of the time with Benj. Smith. On August 8th, 1875 I married Rachel M. Smith, daughter of Benjamin Smith. My father, J.C. Steadman, married us. I had kept company with her for about two months before that. I then thought my first wife dead. I remained at Mr. Smith's not more than 5 months. I then returned to my father's at Elgin. I lived with that lady as my wife until near the close of 1877. Was not at home much of the time. In seven months after August 8th, a son was born. A daughter was born near the close of 1877; I met these children last in March or April, 1878; I was at my father's house when I saw them. We never kept house by ourselves, but were a part of my father's family. To the best of my knowledge she has resided there all the time since we were married, with two exceptions. I was away a great part of the time in various places. Was preaching when away from home. Preached at New Horton, Hillsboro, Alma, Coverdale, Elgin, Washademoic [sic] Lake, and on St. John River. Never preached at Moncton. My business has been preaching when away. When at home I worked upon my farm.

At Kars I lived in the family of James Campbell and was treated very kindly by all the family. I made the acquaintance of Nellie G. Campbell there, and then learned that my wife was alive; and that she was an intimate friend and correspondent of Nellie G.'s. At length I became convinced that she was indeed living. I wrote to her and received a letter from her. I learned that my wife proposed a visit to Kars. This I thought would not answer under the circumstances, and so I informed her that I would meet her at St. John. I did so and remained with her three weeks. I intended to keep her forever ignorant of my connection with Rachel. She was very much pleased to see me, and I rejoiced to see her.

My intimacy at Kars with Nellie G. Campbell had raised a little country scandal there, and so I resigned and went to Georgetown, where I was when I received the invitation to visit the church at Dover. I made arrangements then with my wife [Georgia Ellen] to come to me when I should get settled. I after this wrote a cold, formal letter to my supposed wife [Rachel M. Smith] and sent a small neck chain to the little girl. I corresponded with my wife [Georgia Ellen] while at Georgetown, also with Nellie G. Campbell. I came here [Dover, Maine] and became pastor of the church. I made every effort to keep this matter under, not so much on my own account as that of the children and my supposed wife, thinking it better for them to stand as deserted rather than in the true light. I did not inform my wife of my connection with Rachel Smith because for some time past I have had a growing disposition to believe that a person's confidence would not sustain a very severe test, and I did not wish to try her confidence; she was very delicate and I feared the effect it would have upon her health.

I learned at length that Mr. Campbell was making search for me and would hear the facts. I had arranged to bring my wife to this place [Dover, Maine]. She was to meet me in Bath. I went to Bath and found a letter from her by which I learned that she had learned all the facts about Rachel Smith and refused to come to me.

I received a letter from her father saying if I did not give her up wholly he would expose the whole matter. I sent a despatch addressed to myself in care of H.C. Prentiss, saying my wife had met with an accident and would probably live but a few hours. I then came to Foxcroft again and reported my wife dead. She did virtually die to me that time. H.C. Prentiss wrote a notice of the death for the paper, which he referred to me before publishing. I told him that was about right or would do. I requested my friends not to speak of my wife's death, as it was too painful a subject to me. I have tried in every way to keep the secret, but it has been dragged from me.

I asked people not to speak to me of my wife, as the subject was too painful to me. I referred to the death of my wife in a sermon which caused the people to weep, but I did not weep. Some time in October [1878] I heard of her [actual] death. The second story of her death I set afloat myself. I was grieved at this news. I cannot say at which of these three reports of her death I grieved the most. I have told many falsehoods in this matter which I greatly regret. I have now left off telling falsehoods.

I believed that my wife was dead but did not remarry Rachel Smith for several reasons. I could not do so without exposing the whole matter. I had also learned that she had been false to her vows and had before this resolved that I could not live with her again. I see I have been to blame in this transaction; she only to blame for her infidelity; I last saw Rachel Smith in March or April, 1878; last saw Georgia Campbell, my first wife, in June, 1878 at her father's house where I left her.

My courtship of Miss L. Estelle Gray [of Dover, Maine] commenced sometime in January, 1879, but I had been slightly acquainted with her before; had taken her out to ride before this, but if you call that courtship a great many men court a great many women. I was married to Miss Gray on 23rd of Feb., 1879, by Rev. H.A. Loring.

I went to my uncle's, Dr. John A. Steadman of Georgetown, July 3rd, 1878. I spoke of my [first] wife frequently to him. I don't know that I told him when I married her . . . .

The preacher's uncle, Dr. J.A. Steadman, like the jury, was unsympathetic to his plight. He recounted his July meeting with the bigamist:

I reside in Georgetown, Maine, a physician. C.M. Steadman was at my home in July; he mentioned having a wife; did not say where he married her. I think he had told me something where it

was. I asked him if he was married to Rachel Smith. He replied,
"never, legally."

"Were you married to Nellie Campbell?"

"Yes."

"In 1874?"

"Yes."

"Where does she live?"

"Near Tatmagonch."

"Who married you?"

"Mr. Goucher."

"Magistrate or Minister?"

"A clergyman named Goucher."

I told him I was acquainted with two clergymen by that name,
and I would write and find out if he was telling me the truth. I have
the impression he told me he was a Baptist and resided at Truro,
N.S. He was extremely agitated and begged me not to disclose the
facts.

I charged Steadman with bigamy and upbraided him severely;
told him that his wife was at his father's; that they called her Ray,
that I had found out her name was not Campbell but Smith. He said
that she was not his legal wife. He said he could convince me that
his legal wife was Campbell. That he had a certificate in his trunk
and could show it. I told him that I would not believe a word of
it.

I asked him why he had asked me in his letter to lie for him.
He said he knew it was no use as soon as he had written it. With
all his weeping I had no confidence in him and told him so. I
threatened to get an officer and have him detained, but he begged
me not to do so. He said he only wanted to get away and he could
prove his innocence if he had a chance and that he was legally
married to Miss Gray. I advised him to leave the country, to take
a ship and go to Europe, for they would follow him and have him
arrested if he did not leave the country.

I told him about his mother. She was almost dead through his
conduct. He wept genuine tears when I told him of his mother. He

was deeply affected but did not move me much. He said, "Oh my God, what shall I do, what shall I do?" I told him to shoot himself — to put a pistol to his head and blow his brains out. If I had had a pistol with me then I think I should have given it to him I was so disgusted with him.

It was a question in my mind if he was insane or on the borders of it. He seemed to have no sense or reason at times. I expressed my doubt of his sanity to my family when I got home. I read a letter from him, requesting J.A. Steadman to write H.C. Prentiss at Foxcroft, stating that his wife died at his house; that he brought her home from the Province; that his name was on the minutes as an ordained minister, and that he was what he had represented himself to be. Letter was dated 8th of May, 1879.

(*The Moncton Daily Times*, 22 September 1879)

STREET CORNER LOAFING:
"A NUISANCE THAT MUST BE ABATED"

Charlottetown, in the late 1800s, was a community of some 11,000 residents, policed by a Force totalling fewer than 10 officers. As in other Maritime communities, the most common offence was public drunkenness. Petty crime — including theft, burglary, and common assault — challenged the supposed peace and harmony of this Island town. The police, aided by an assortment of temperance groups, battled unsuccessfully to enforce the Scott Act. The illegal liquor trade continued to flourish in the 1880s. The Stipendiary Magistrate's Court reflected the prosaic nature of crime. Each day's docket contained the usual assortment of drunk and disorderlies, assaults and minor thefts.

One persistent problem for the police in Charlottetown, as elsewhere in the region, was the "street corner loafing nuisance." Young men held court on city corners, using abusive language, becoming embroiled in fights and rowdy activities and harrassing passersby. A July weekend in 1878 was marred by the presence of these "loafers." Late Saturday night "a crowd of roughs assembled at the corner of Water and Great George Streets and engaged in a most determined fight, holding undisputed sway for nearly an hour" (*The Daily Examiner*, 8 July 1878). The next night the same crowd of youths assembled; their oaths and obscenities loudly echoed across city streets. The police were routinely criticized for not effectively controlling this threat to public order.

In December the corner loafing nuisance appeared to abate briefly, with the sentencing of four of the "chief props to Hyndman's corner" (*The Daily Examiner*, 11 December 1878). Two were given three months in jail with hard labor. Yet this was not viewed as erasing the problem; a gang of twenty-five other "vagrant corner

Charlottetown, 1890s (PAPEI)

loafers" were at large. One Michael Began was brought before the Magistrate for being a "perpetual corner loafer." He escaped the fate of his companions, as the charge was not substantiated. Began was able to show that "he worked when he could get work to do" (*The Daily Examiner,* 13 December 1878). Corner loafing and vagrancy were, in the minds of authorities, closely linked. Offenders were at times described as "street arabs." Not uncommonly they were charged with theft, as happened to John Doyle in June, 1879, when he was arrested for having stolen a large number of articles from vehicles standing at the market. Loafing and vagrancy were seen as contributing to Charlottetown's street crime. Though periodically criticized for their inaction, the police did at times seek to respond to this "menace":

> A gang of disorderly fellows who infest the various corners of the city were, yesterday, raided by the police. A small number was arrested. They appeared before the Stipendiary this forenoon, when that official rightfully pronounced on each a meritorious sentence for their many many offences. Alfred Farmer, a boy about fourteen years of age, was very drunk when arrested. He is a noted

young vagrant, and the Magistrate sent him up for four
months, with hard labor. John Brogan, a boy seemingly
the same age as Farmer, was also drunk at the time of arrest. He will accompany Farmer for 20 days. James
Goodman and Daniel McDonald, two well known corner
loafers, were each sentenced to two months with hard
labor for vagrancy . . . .

(The Daily Examiner, 4 July 1879)

The Court, too, sought to curb the activities of gangs of
"roughs," at times by ordering them to leave the city. At least one
such troublesome youth exited with some enthusiasm:

Patrick Brogan, John Bowden, and John Ready were
charged with keeping company with a gang of thieves
and also wandering the city at unreasonable hours of the
night. The trio denied the charge "in toto," and after
giving a brief account of their respective stewardships
they were discharged with the warning that if they were
again arrested on such a charge they would be imprisoned
for three months with hard labor. Ready was further ordered to leave the city within 24 hours. He to all ap-
pearances thanked the Magistrate for his kindness, and
remarked that if he could catch him in the city tomorrow
he might imprison him forever.

(The Daily Examiner, 16 September 1879)

Despite the halting efforts of authorities to deal with the street
crime — corner loafing and disturbances, vandalism, theft —
caused by youths, Charlottetown was getting a reputation as a
"centre of rowdyism." The call for corporal punishment and for
even a reformatory was heard from the citizenry. Such suggestions
did little to remedy the problem.

In February, 1880, the attention of the police was again drawn
to the increased number of corner loafers and their predilection
toward insulting the numerous ladies who passed their "infested
places." One of Charlottetown's respected gentlemen, reflecting a
sense of impatience with the situation, placed a rather pointed
advertisement:

Wanted — Two or three policemen to disperse gangs of roughs who meet at the corners on Prince Street on Sabbath evenings. These roughs may be found from the upper corner on Judge Young's grounds to the Atheneum. They cause ladies and others much annoyance as they frequently blockade the way.

(*The Daily Examiner*, 1 March 1880)

Such a plea was ineffective. The corner loafers, disparagingly categorized as "hoodlums," continued to congregate nightly on the corners from Queen to Prince Streets and at other public places in the city. To curb the "epidemic," authorities were urged to make examples of those "unprincipled scoundrels" who were brought before the Court. This advice was periodically heeded, as in March, 1880, when five "hoodlums" were sentenced to six weeks' imprisonment with hard labor. The Magistrate, in sentencing them, remarked that when their time expired, they would either have to discontinue corner loafing or leave the country. These threats did little to curb the problem.

Corner loafers were the source of more than incidents of disorderly behavior on Charlottetown's streets. These "young roughs" were not averse to actual physical attacks on passersby. For this they were strongly condemned but also undoubtedly feared:

On Saturday evening last, about dusk, two inoffensive young men, employees of the Woolen Factory, were attacked by some of our corner roughs, and badly beaten near Mr. P. Connolly's, on Queen Square. It is about time that our citizens made up their minds as to who is to have charge of the town, the civic authorities and police, or the corner loafers. Almost every day we hear complaints of assaults upon, and insulting language used to, persons passing along, by these worthless fellows who infest almost every corner on Queen Street. It is a nuisance that must be abated. The Police know the names of the offenders without further information.

(*The Daily Examiner*, 27 July 1881)

The loafers showed contempt toward the police. When asked to move along by a constable, they would return to their "post" when he had left. Passing ladies continued to be exposed to their impudent stares and coarse voices. Men, women and children were abused, sometimes physically. The police, again, launched raids; but the "nuisance" abated only temporarily. Efforts to curb the loafers at times interfered with the activities of more law-abiding citizens:

> I would like to ask why it is that there is no discrimination made between a common loafer and the cab-driver who is waiting on business at the station, or why it is that he is thrust out of the waiting room because some loafers happen to be in there and get chewing tobacco and squirting saliva over the floor. It is strange that the keeper of the room cannot keep the loafers out without compelling those who are on business to leave the room, and in consequence have to wait outside in the cold until arrival of the train. It is bad enough to have one's horse out for half an hour or an hour in the cold, especially when it is not the most agreeable weather, without one's own person being so exposed . . . .
>
> (*The Daily Examiner*, 6 March 1882)

At least some of the corner loafers and "street arabs" were well known to the police; they *were* distinguished from the respectable citizenry, and dealt with accordingly:

> Andy Brown, a noted young street arab and vagrant was, a short time ago, ordered by the Stipendiary Magistrate to leave the city and remain away until he had his Christmas dinner prepared for him. Andy couldn't. On Saturday he came to the city, and as usual, got up to his eyes in mischief. He saw the office of Theoph Stewart, Esq. open, and waited until he had left the apartment, then entering he locked the door on the inside, and proceeded to investigate. Mr. Stewart returned and saw what was passing. He notified the police and brave Andy

was arrested. To-day Andy was ordered to find a situation in the country or go to jail for four months. He has not yet decided whether work in the country or cheap lodging all winter is to him most acceptable.

(*The Daily Examiner*, 19 November 1883)

What is striking about this "nuisance" was its persistence in Charlottetown through the 1880s. The problem may have waned periodically, but returned with the accompanying condemnation that its presence inspired. In late November of 1883 the corner loafing nuisance was described as worse than ever:

Stationed at all the corners from the Apothecaries Hall down to the Atheneum and from Dr. Dodd's down to the extreme end of Queen Street may be seen nightly a crowd of loafers, whose only purpose in life seems to be to insult passersby. Could not the police be induced to look after these individuals and if possible to keep them on the move. Another rendez-vous of this class of individuals is at Dawson's corner, where especially on Sunday nights things are pretty lively by their playful pranks and the somewhat coarse nature of their language.

(*The Daily Examiner,* 28 November 1883)

In July of the following year the police and Magistrate were again castigated for their apparent ineffectiveness in resolving the problem:

Of late the police have given little attention to the corner loafing nuisance. The consequence is that the denizens who spend their nights in the dark haunts in different parts of the town have become bold and insulting. Last night a gentleman quietly passing a gang of those hoodlums was grossly insulted. The epithets used were the foulest which could emanate from the throat of a demon, but in this law abiding city he was obliged to bear with it, owing to the absence of officers of the law. Not only do they insult gentlemen, but ladies are obliged to either leave the street or hold their ears to escape filthy, disgusting, disgraceful language, used night after night by these

Queen Street, Charlottetown, 1890s. (PAPEI)

incarnate fiends. We hope that the Magistrate will direct
his men to give closer attention to this nuisance which
appears to be chronic and punish the offenders as they
rightfully deserve. We suggest "the cat" as a proper
remedy.

(The Daily Examiner, 15 July 1884)

The call for more decided action against these "incarnate
fiends" was repeated in subsequent years. In March of 1888 the
police were instructed to "keep a close eye after corner loafers," reflecting the apparent prominence of the nuisance over the
preceding several months. That they continued to interfere with the
orderly routine of business and of services in the city was apparent:

Now that the police vacancies are filled up, doubtless the
loafing nuisance will receive the attention of that force.
There is, however, one especial form of this disorder on
exhibition in the post office delivery hall, whenever a
large late mail is being wicketed to applicants. It is sometimes a considerable difficulty to find passing room, but
that would be a small matter if the crowd was not swelled
by obstructing loafers, who only assemble because they
have no business there. Could not the new police be instructed to make all "move on" after getting their mail,

and the Postmaster be induced to put his "notice to quit" the premises while the mail is being given out as soon as possible . . . .

(The Daily Examiner, 13 September 1888)

Residents of the neighborhood around Fitzroy and Edward Streets in February, 1889, complained vociferously of the corner loafing nuisance there. The police were blamed for this in a more personal and individual manner than was typically the case:

Although an officer of the law lives in the neighborhood, the nuisance goes on unabated. People do not understand how it is that this is the case, although some think it is owing to the fact of his residence not fronting on the street. However this may be, the general impression is that the officer should either move his residence or the loafers.

(The Daily Examiner, 5 February 1889)

When it could do so, the Court continued to express condemnation of the problem. On a June morning in 1892, four boys were charged with corner loafing and annoying persons in their dwellings. They received fines from $1 or 4 days to $5 or 30 days. "In giving judgment His Honour commented severely upon the prevalence of corner-loafing, and said he would take strong steps to remedy the evil" *(The Daily Examiner*, 3 June 1891). The next day several young lads wanted by the police for corner loafing and annoying residents in their dwellings made haste to leave the city, perhaps taking heed of the Magistrate's warning.

That the problem of corner loafing persisted through these years suggests that public order was not necessarily secure on Charlottetown's streets. The "loafers" appeared to have been predominantly male youths, native to the city, without stable employment but free of the constraining influence of their families. The police, as they did with violators of the Canada Temperance Act, sought periodically to enforce the law, but perhaps recognized that they could at best only contain the problem rather than eliminate it entirely. The calls for a return to the whip, for the establishment of a reformatory, for the imposition of a sentence with hard labor, for forced removal from the community, were expressions of the continued sense of frustration found among authorities and the "respectable citizenry" in responding effectively to this "nuisance." That the "loafers" also became embroiled in assault, theft, damage to property, and interfered with the daily business and service activities in the city heightened the recognition that this was more than a simple nuisance. At the same time, their verbal assault on Charlottetown's wives and daughters offended moral sensitivities and thus from time to time stimulated equally strong condemnation. If street corner loafing was indeed a "nuisance that must be abated," its persistence underscored the difficulty Maritime communities had in banishing petty crime from their streets in the late nineteenth century.

RELIGIOUS ARMIES
AND THE THREAT TO PEACE

In the 1880s Charlottetown was visited by religious "armies" intent on renewing the Christian allegiance of the fallen and those wavering in faith. The Salvation Army and the rival Gospel Army counted Charlottetown, much to the chagrin of the established churches, as one of the "fields" in which lost souls (especially those of the lower classes) must be regained. This missionary effort, insofar as it invoked debate, criticism and to some degree disorder, was problematic for both police and citizenry.

That the Salvation Army differed from the more formal, less emotive ceremonies of the major churches was evident to any observer of its ceremonies:

> The Salvation Army on Sunday had its usual muster, procession, kneel drill, and attack on Satan's kingdom. The muster took place at the Barracks, Little Richmond Street, at 7:15, Lieut. Nellie Kiezer in command. At that time there were about 100 persons in the Hall. Children were running up and down the gallery steps where the soldiers sit, the fifer was engaged in trying a few of his favourite airs. A boy with a mysterious instrument of awful discord, called the ocarina, was making the place hideous with din, soldiers were chattering merrily, a girl with the tambourine now and again manifested her deftness with that peculiar instrument, the cymbals added their quota to their unharmonious proceeding, and the scraping of fiddles out of tune completed the mixture of discordant sounds. At last some kind of order was brought out of the chaos, the band struck up a lively tune, and a few soldiers followed with

When the battle's over,
We shall wear a crown
In the New Jerusalem.

Lieut. Kiezer now entered the barracks, rapidly marched up the aisle, gave the tambourine a dexterous thrump, advanced to the front, knelt down, and prayed briefly that the Lord would be with them in their parade, give them a good meeting, and save precious souls. The procession was then formed and the streets were paraded. When the party returned Lieut. Kiezer commenced

My sins are washed away
By the blood of the Lamb.

The triangle chimed in slowly, the fiddles doubtingly follow, and cymbals crash in, but still there was an evident lagging. All the soldiers were not singing, and only a few of the audience joined in. The leader then called for "knee drill," and her invocation was direct to the point. "Oh, Lord," said she, "we are glad we are here tonight. We are glad we are in Thy company. We are glad to be with Jesus, and we ask Thee to come right down among us. Oh, God Almighty, come in our midst tonight. Oh come in our midst tonight and save sinners here. Oh come tonight and speak right to their hearts and wash away all their sins. Help them Lord to come to Thee tonight, and confess Thee before this meeting, and take right hold of Thee by faith. Oh, Lord, save souls tonight here for Jesus sake." Lieut. Nellie Keizer then mounted the platform and commenced singing:

I heard the voice of Jesus say
Come unto Me and rest.

She was dressed in a tight-fitting scarlet cloth jacket, [which] if, it did not show her to be the "glass of fashion," demonstrated that she was not far from the "mould of form." Several more players followed, interspersed with various songs which were more or less heartily joined in by the audience.

29

The Lieutenant then announced that she would read Isaiah iv., and in doing so she interspersed remarks. "Seek ye the Lord while he may be found. You will wish some day that you had come if you neglect this great Salvation. Come now tonight, while you are in your health and strength, and seek the Lord. I am glad He is here tonight — bless him (amen). For my thoughts are not your thoughts, neither are your ways My ways. Now, there are a great many of you want to get saved in your own way. It may be right at home, when nobody but you and God are there; but Jesus says here, 'My ways are not your ways.' Oh call on Jesus tonight and get saved. 'The mountains and the hills shall break forth before you into singing, all the trees of the field shall clap their hands.' That will be a noisy meeting when the mountains start into singing and the trees clap their hands. You think the Salvation Army is noisy, but when we get up yonder there we will then start into shouting."

The Lieutenant then gave out the announcement relating to the first anniversary of the Salvation Army in Canada, and asked for contributions in jink. "The people will be hungry," said she, "and I want you to send on your contributions, no matter what it is, and the Lord will bless you. You [who] come here Sunday after Sunday are getting good all the time, and you ought to send something, no matter what it is — a barrel of flour, a cow or a pig. (Laughter). If you cannot send something give us some money. We Salvation folks haven't got a cent — I know I haven't — and you people have got to pay for those barracks." A dollar was handed up, and for a time the giving flagged. "Be careful that God don't make you pay a great doctor's ill, for you know that all that you got belongs to him." The money came a little more freely, and she sang:

Roll the old chariot along.
If the devil's in the way roll it over him.

Experiences were then the order of the day, and a soldier of three weeks' standing gave an intelligent
statement of his experience, and strongly urged the many
young men in the audience who knew him to give their
hearts to Jesus. Another exhorted singers to give the Lord
a trial, "for," said he, "the devil will take you back any
time you want to go." Another said he was a faithful
backslider — "a backslider from the devil. I believe the
devil has got very little show among the Salvation Army.
The Lord can save everybody, and if the devil was to turn
God would save him." After these expressions an assault
was made on the people, the Army was spread out in
skirmishing order,

What wonders God to us hath given,
Salvation wires reach to heaven

was sung, and a general jubilee closed the proceedings.
The hall was about three-fourths full, this comparatively
small attendance being due possibly to the fact that there
was a silver collection at the door.

(*The Daily Examiner*, 3 September 1883)

The Salvation Army meetings were frequently well attended. In
late March, 1886, the barracks proved too small to accommodate
those who sought admission. The crowd was moved temporarily to
the Market Hall (itself seen indeed as "the enemy's fortifications");
even there it was overflowing. Yet not all were to find the war on
the wages of sin to be equally attractive.

The Salvation Army was not alone in this "war." A small band
of workers, calling themselves the Gospel Army and originating in
Saint John, arrived in Charlottetown in October of 1885. The local
"detachment" included Capt. J.H. Collins, Miss Bartlett and Mrs.
Weeks. The Gospel Army saw itself as distinct from the Salvation
Army:

Its aim is to teach not only the unconverted but also those
who take no active interest in the churches. The meetings
are held at such hours as not to interfere with the different churches. They are held in Public Halls, so as to

have it as undenominational as possible, and also that any Christian may have perfect liberty and freedom to take part in the services, and because many will come who will not attend the churches. Converts are always recommended to join the church of their own choice. This Army differs from the Salvation Army in that the Salvation Army organize permanently and are separate and distinct from the churches, and hold services at the same hour as the churches. While adopting many of the methods of the Salvation Army, they omit the use of drums and flags and other of the more prominent features . . . .

(*The Daily Examiner,* 12 October 1885)

The Gospel Army meetings were held most frequently at the Academy of Music, where a special gallery was reserved for the ladies attending. This separation, it is of interest to note, was adopted to improve the order of their meetings. Like its counterpart, the Gospel Army did not restrict its activities to within a hall; parades, for example to the Market Square, were regular occurrences.

Yet these meetings were not necessarily peaceful encounters with the Lord or with the "saved." The war on sin was marked by periodic reminders that these religious armies must march a road marked with confrontation and conflict:

A panic occurred in the Salvation Army Barracks on Wednesday night which terminates in the Stipendiary Magistrate's Court this forenoon. It appears that about 9 o'clock that evening one of the soldiers was telling the large assemblage present how he had been rescued from the thraldom of sin through the beneficent office of the Army. A man in the audience who evidently did not take much stock in the story of conversion cried out to the soldier to "shut up." The noise started the people in the gallery who suspecting that a row had broken out in the body of the barracks rushed downstairs, breaking the bannister in their flight and creating a panic among the women. While this had been going on the man had been taken outside by the police. Yesterday morning a complaint was made against him by Capt. Cook, and this forenoon the case came before the Court. Witnesses were examined who identified the defendant as the man who shouted, and after being lectured by His Honour he was fined $10 or one month's imprisonment.

(The Daily Examiner, 14 May 1886)

During the progress of a holiness meeting at the Salvation Army Barracks, last evening, the janitor, Albert Allin, who was in charge of the door, deemed it necessary to go outside the building and inform some young men who were on the platform that they had better stop making a noise, as they were disturbing the meeting. The young men evidently did not take kindly to Allin's advice, and one of them stepped forward, and telling Allin not to shove him, struck him a violent blow over the left eye, cutting and blacking it. Allin says he was struck with a steel knuckle. After being struck, Allin started for the doctor's to have his injured eye dressed, but had not proceeded far when he was overtaken by the same young men and again beaten. When picked up by a fellow Salvationist and a friend later on Allin was insensible. His assailants will probably figure at the Police Court in the course of a few days.

(The Daily Examiner, 15 November 1890)

A buxom Salvation Army soldier got into difficulties with some young men, and was prohibited by the Captain from going on the saved platform with the other soldiers. This ruffled her usually placid temper, and with a peculiar display of Christian toleration she had a young man, whom she accused of assaulting her on Sunday night last, arraigned before the Stipendiary Magistrate today. The plaintiff was placed upon the stand and took the oath with considerable unctiousness. She stated that on Sunday evening last, about twenty minutes to ten, after the services of the army had been concluded, she left the barracks for her residence. On her way she was accosted by two young men, one of whom actually had the audacity to catch her by the arm. The young men walked along, one on each side of her and amused themselves by trying to push her off the sidewalk as well as by using language which she considered indecent and which jarred greatly upon her usually sensitive organism. She only knew one of the young men and consequently only had one summoned. The defendant on oath denied the charge brought against him. Several witnesses, among whom were two soldiers of the Army, and the young man's companion, testified that beyond the fact of the woman being "seen home" by the two young men there was no truth whatever in her story. The Magistrate, after announcing that he was disgusted with the whole affair, dismissed the case.

(*The Daily Examiner*, 10 June 1886)

That these meetings were accompanied by disturbances, fights and at least some disorder, incited at least partly by youths less intent on salvation than on mischief, both inside the hall and on the streets, drew the ire of Charlottetown's citizens:

Sir, — In the East End it appears the saved from the Salvation Army invaded the infernal regions in hell street last evening to the utter disgust of the Dennison's. A free fight ensued in which the saved came out second best and the victors retain the saved's banners as trophies. All this happened on Sunday evening . . . the Army's parades are disgraceful. What disorderly band of costumed lunatics would be permitted to disturb the peace of the city in the way this so-called Army carries on. Certainly there is nothing respectable in it. At the most it is a source of amusement for the foolish youth in the streets and a source of still greater evil in packing a mocking, laugh-

ing, jeering crowd of loose characters in the barracks at
night. The Army officers, from the recital of their own
experiences (and half is not told) are anything but good.
Their conduct is anything but modest. They are admit-
tedly loose fish and are offering a rendezvous for
thoughtless youngsters and old fools at night. Much evil
has come of these meetings thus far and much more will
yet be experienced. Let the unbeliever keep his eye on
the returns of illegitimate births for the year ending 31st
of December next. But to come back to the East End
troubles, no doubt these young fellows will be before His
Honour tomorrow for disturbing those angels of peace
. . . . A corner loafer or drunk would get two dollars or
8 days. A disturber of such mercenaries must needs fork
out 30 dollars or go down for a month. Surely the scales
of justice are unevenly balanced. Surely it is time to
employ officers of the law in something better than
giving protection to such characters. Surely it is time for
parents of any respectability to awaken to the terrible risk
they run in allowing their children to attend such disreputable assemblies as Salvation meetings.

"Common Decency"
(The Daily Examiner, 20 April 1887)

Especially irksome were the parades the Salvation Army and
Gospel Army mounted through city streets. That they occurred on
Sunday and, at least in the case of the former, were accompanied
by singing and the playing of musical instruments, seemed an additional irritant. Confrontations with the police seemed inevitable, as
threatened to be the case in late June, 1886:

Many prominent citizens are taking exception to the Sunday parades of the Salvation Army. On Saturday evening
an officer of the law waited upon Captain Cook and, after
informing her of this fact, requested that in future the
Sunday parade be discontinued. The Captain and the
Army had as much right to play their drums and parade
the streets on Sunday as the churches had to ring their

bells; consequently, she could not accede to the request to discontinue the parade. Yesterday afternoon a report was abroad that the Army was to be arrested, and large numbers gathered in the neighborhood of the police station to "see the fun." About half-past two the beating of drums and the clashing of cymbals was heard in the direction of the Barracks. The excitement became more intense, and the crowd near the police station was soon largely augmented. Nearer and nearer came the red-shirted recruits. Several policemen were in the Station door, and the eyes of the multitude, as the Army approached them, were upon them. At length the Army arrived opposite the Station, and just when it was expected that the "grand raid" would take place, the Salvationists, looking quizzically at the policemen, started up "We'll fight — we'll fight!" etc., as loudly as possible, accompanied by the playing of drums and marched past — unharmed. The disappointed crowd followed the Army to the Square where the open air service was held, which on this particular occasion was even more demonstrative than usual. The day's proceedings were brought to a close with a grand "free and easy" in the barracks.

(*The Daily Examiner*, 28 June 1886)

Little comfort could be taken in reports from New Haven, London, Springhill, Quebec and Halifax, that efforts at least there were being made to ban Salvation Army Sunday parades on city streets. Charlottetown's police, as the supposed guardians of public order, themselves did not escape criticism:

Sir, — ... The city maintains a force of six "portly and handsome" policemen to guard it day and night. It is but reasonable to suppose that, like other mortals, policemen require rest and refreshment, so we may assume that, at most, one half the force are on duty at one time; the other half being off for rest, held in reserve or on special duty. Now, as never less than two of our policemen are to be seen at any of the meetings of the Salvation Army, and as one man is required for "station duty," the question presents itself who patrols the town? Perhaps we may thus account for prisoners, sometimes, being able to walk unhindered out of the police station, and if it is a "cold day" taking the stove along with them. We gain, perhaps, by knowing now, where to find a policeman when one is wanted.

Yours, etc.
Vigilance.
(The Daily Examiner, 18 May 1886)

That more attention seemed to be paid to corner loafers and the street "roughs" than to these religious demonstrations was a cry heard more than once:

Sir, — I have twice refrained from making a complaint in the press against the disorderly proceedings of Salvationists (so-called) on Queen Square, because I was in hopes that the authorities would check them; but it seems that His Honour the Stipendiary Magistrate is so zealous for the salvation of souls that he is willing to endanger the lives of citizens by allowing this howling nuisance to continue.

Some months ago, while passing up Queen Street with a funeral, as undertaker, these people created such an uproar that it was with the greatest difficulty I succeeded in controlling my horses. Some time afterwards I had occasion to pass the same place, as undertaker, and met with the same difficulty. Last Sunday evening, while passing Queen Square in charge of the remains of the late D. McMillan, the same commotion prevailed, and again I barely succeeded in preventing a runaway.

The experience of this city in paying damages should, I think, open the eyes of the authorities to a sense of the danger they are incurring by allowing this state of things to continue. Assuredly, if these demonstrations are not discontinued, there will be another large bill to pay out of the public chest some fine morning.

These good people create more disturbance and cause more anxiety than all the roughs in the city, and it would be a nice question to decide which of the two classes indulge most in blasphemy; but instead of punishing the "warriors," they are encouraged with legal protection which continually endangers the lives of citizens.

Michael Hennessy
(*The Daily Examiner*, 16 February 1889)

Perhaps more fundamental to the community's reaction to the activities of the "armies" was the belief that they departed too far from, and indeed competed with, the religious standards of the established churches. This version of religion was not that of the respectable citizenry. For some it was a travesty:

Everybody knows something at least about the Salvation Army. In the declared aim of the army there is everything to recommend, in the workings of the army there is much to criticize and perhaps censure. Caution should be observed before one should inveigh against eccentricities in a worker for the promotion of God's cause. It is acknowledged that often certain classes are reached through unexpected and most peculiar means. And when some poor soul is lifted up from the depths of degradation through a strange instrumentality, there is reason to praise the Lord. The workings of the Salvation Army are somewhat novel, yet good results have followed. This is a delightful enthusiasm which takes possession of the new-born child of God, but often human frailty gets the upper hand, and mingling with the enthusiasm produces fanaticism. It was time the Salvation Army was coming to the consciousness that irreverence of thought, of word, and of work is out of place when seeking to do the Lord's work. In one of the army's programmes for a week in June was read the following heading:

"War! War! And an invitation to everybody to join in the fight against Old Nick."

Then comes the following: —

Monday — Salvation charge.

Tuesday — Great exhibition of Hallelujah lasses.

Wednesday — Fire and brimstone.

Thursday — Roll-call; soldiers to deliver up their cartridges.

Friday — Baptism of fire.

Saturday — Rejoicing over victories won.

All over the shop meetings.

Sunday, 7 a.m. — Knee drill; ammunition supplied by Quartermaster General.

11 a.m. — Descent of the Holy Ghost.

2:30 p.m. — Tremendous Free-and-Easy.

6:30 p.m. — Great charge on the Devil.

9:00 p.m. — Hallelujah Gallop.

Now this is making a travesty out of religion. It is shockingly irreverent. It is turning religion into a farce. Some, indeed many, of the warmest Christians in the Old Land, who helped the movement at first, are lifting their voices in emphatic condemnation of the ridiculous element that is becoming so prominent. And here in our New Land, when every true-hearted disciple is glad when sinners are converted and regenerated, it is not too soon to make known to the new workmen that in carrying out God's work, while enthusiasm and hallowed fervour are pleasing to him, irreverence is highly displeasing.

(The Daily Examiner, 19 August 1882)

Opponents of these sects attacked them for their irreverence and fanaticism. They could also find in such adherents as Margaret Lisle Shepherd a rationale for distrusting their sincerity and virtue:

Margaret Lisle Shepherd, née Miss Herbert, well-known in Charlottetown from her connection with the defunct Gospel Army, is still posing as a "converted nun" in the United States. At latest accounts she was "doing" Pennsylvania. Here is what occurred at one of her recent lectures in York, as related in a despatch of the 19th: Mrs. Margaret Shepherd of Boston lectured here yesterday and last night on the Roman Catholic Church. The woman professes to be a converted Romanist. On leaving the hall, accompanied by her husband last night, she was hit by a stone thrown by Victor Segner. She was stunned and badly frightened. The force of the stone was broken by a knot of ribbon on her hat. Policemen Wire and Truett chased Segner, but the former sprained his ankle. Truett, after calling on Segner to stop without effect, shot at him, the ball hitting him in the left side and coming out near the heart. It is not known how serious the wound is.

(*The Daily Examiner*, 25 March 1890)

The emotionality and unconventionality of these sects appealed to some in Charlottetown. For many, however, the religious armies were a source of disorder. Their threat was to the peace and order of the community; but it was also to institutionalized religion.

THE CALLAGHAN MURDER

On Sunday, May 24th, 1885, John Longworth found something peculiar at Sherwood Cemetery, on the outskirts of Charlottetown. Driving up, he noticed that the keeper, an old man named James Callaghan (a native of County Monaghan, Ireland, who had come to P.E.I. seventeen years earlier) had left a basket and garden tools outside where it appeared he had been planting potatoes. Not seeing Callaghan, Longworth entered his lodge. Potato sets were laid in a basket behind the door and were dried up as if they had been cut three or four days earlier. The kitchen was in disarray; beans and peas were scattered all over the floor. The scene was equally puzzling in the bedroom, where bedclothes had been thrown on the floor. The silence echoed as Longworth shouted for the keeper. After inspecting the out-house to see if he was there, the neighbor left with some concern.

Three days later, perhaps encouraged by his father's solicitude, young Brenton Longworth entered Callaghan's house after he received no answer as he knocked at the door. He could not ignore a fearful stench. In the bedroom he, too, found the bedclothes on the floor. This time a black cat sat on top of them. Kicking the animal away, he moved the bedclothes and discovered the body of a man lying face downwards, with an arm around the leg of a table. The youth noticed blood on the right hand of the body. The walls also were spattered with blood in a few places near the body. In panic he ran out and drove around the cemetery before returning to the house, perhaps to see if indeed what greeted him minutes earlier was not an illusion.

Longworth immediately drove into Charlottetown to summon the coroner and Marshal Flynn. When they arrived a crowd had already gathered. What they discovered shocked even the coroner. The murdered man lay face down with his legs doubled up. His skull had been fractured, his throat cut. A sharp wound marked the back of his right hand. Walls, floor and ceiling were spattered with blood — all fruits of the violent struggle that had obviously occurred.

The Marshal searched the house and discovered the "deadly instruments." A large, blunt knife covered with blood was found on the kitchen table. In addition, an iron gate bar and a potato pounder, also covered with blood, were retrieved from the cellar. Flynn's first thoughts were that more than one man had committed the murder, but he quickly recognized that this could have been the work of a lone assailant.

A formal inquest was subsequently held. After hearing several weeks of testimony, the coroner's jury concluded that the deceased had been killed by some unknown party or parties. The identity of the latter was expected to be confirmed when two youths from Rustico Road were arrested after information was provided that they had used threatening language towards Callaghan a short time before the murder. This expectation was premature. Arraigned before the Stipendiary Magistrate, the youths were able to provide evidence that they could not have been near the cemetery when the crime occurred. The "long arm of the law" next pointed to one Alexander Gillis, who had been arrested at Harmony Station for larceny, and was found to have in his possession the murdered man's watch, chain and gold piece. Such incriminating evidence could not be ignored. In late January, 1886, Gillis was put on trial.

Gillis was no stranger to such proceedings. Born in Arisaig, Nova Scotia, in 1851, he moved with his family to Georgetown, P.E.I., after his father's shipbuilding business had failed. Their stay in Georgetown was not a lengthy one; a year later they moved permanently to Charlottetown where the family lived rather modestly. Tired of the odd jobs he was only able to obtain, the son left the city to work as a farm hand in Royalty and at East Point. When he reached the age of eighteen, young Alexander decided to make a more drastic change, from which point his moral demise could be charted. He left the Island entirely to work as a fisherman and coaster at Gloucester, Massachusetts. Thrown in with "lawless characters," it was not long before he learned the rhythm of work — drunkenness — sobriety; work — drunkenness — . . . . Five or six years' exposure to this pattern left him a rather hardened individual, whose fate would eventually lead to a confrontation with authorities. Such occurred while he was under the influence of liquor. In league with another, equally insensitized by drink, Gillis robbed a man on a highway. For this crime he was sentenced to six years' imprisonment. His stay in prison seemed ameliorative; officials found his behavior praiseworthy and relieved him of all hard labor. So impressed were they, that he was appointed a sub-warden over the condemned prisoners. In time his term of imprisonment was shortened by one year, and he was released in 1881. It was quickly evident that his conversion had been short-lived. His passion for drink and for dissolute companions regained its hold. Several months later he was convicted of burglary and was returned to prison to serve a three-year term. Again his conduct there was exemplary. Authorities seemed blind to his previous demonstration of a failed conversion, for once more they shortened his sentence. Now in ill health, Gillis returned to the Island in 1884 and stayed with his sister at Harmony, in Kings County, where he again worked as a farm hand in the Royalty and at a nearby lobster factory. His previous experiences very clearly left their mark; he continued to indulge in liquor and, neighbours reported, when under the influence was given to bullying the more timid.

Not all found him repulsive. After his return to Harmony, Gillis took up with a young woman, Mary Ellen MacDonald, who lived with her parents four miles away. As the girl later recounted, Gillis could not keep away from her, despite her mother's disapproval. The suitor gained such disfavour, it appeared, partly because he never attended church. His misdeeds became even more marked when the girl gave birth to his illegitimate child in November, 1885. As Gillis waited for his trial, the young woman continued to express her affection and loyalty in the numerous letters she wrote him. Seeing nothing good in the letters Gillis himself wrote back, the girl's mother burned them before they could be read. What encouragement Gillis took from the letters he received was unknown. That he recognized the evidence against him was compelling was revealed in one letter which did get delivered to the young woman: he entreated that she seek to prove that he was at her place the day of the murder.

The quest for an alibi was fruitless. The Crown carefully pieced together the testimony of a variety of witnesses who were able to establish the location of Gillis during the week of the murder. Although the body had been discovered on May 27th it was obvious the murder had occurred some days previous to that. The assailant himself had unwittingly helped authorities to fix the exact date of the assault. Callaghan, as it was noted, had been that day out in the garden planting potatoes. His body was found covered by the bedclothes the killer had thrown over it; the clothes the deceased wore thus retained moisture. With the help of local officials who kept meteorological records it was established that the murder must have occurred on May 20th. For that day it rained. It remained, then, to determine where Gillis had been before, during, and after the murder.

The week previous to the murder, it was substantiated, Gillis was at Harmony, fifty miles from Charlottetown. May 15th was election day for the county. The accused came to the MacDonald home that evening but did not stay long. Instead he went off to a nearby party, perhaps joining in the celebration of the results. Returning to the MacDonald's homestead, he stayed there Saturday night. About noon the next day he left, saying he was going to his brother John's, intending the next morning to take the train to Charlottetown. Perhaps preparing for his misdeed, Gillis shaved off his moustache while en route to Mount Stewart. Arriving in the city, he went to the North Star Hotel, using the name McInnis. The proprietor's suspicion was raised when the stranger seemed unacquainted with the McInnis family at Harmony. That suspicion strengthened when on Wednesday Gillis left, saying he was taking the train back, but forgetting to pay his bill. The hotel keeper, Duncan McMillan, went down to the station to locate Gillis but without success. The Crown argued that Gillis instead went to the cemetery and there murdered Callaghan. The following day, Gillis appeared at Mount Stewart where he made a fatal mistake. Approaching the station master, Horace McEwen, he asked that a gold coin, which it was later confirmed had belonged to the murdered man, be changed, as he wanted to purchase some articles. McEwen obliged, and an additional piece of circumstantial evidence was subsequently identified. Two days after the murder Gillis again appeared at Harmony. Mrs. MacDonald recalled that at the time he appeared especially anxious:

> . . . He was at our place when I came home. I did not notice any change in his appearance that night. He was sitting in a dark place behind the door. He did not sleep at our house that night but came back the next day and stayed about an hour, from 10 till 11 o'clock. I noticed him coming in through the kitchen. I went upstairs, and while I was up in the loft I heard awful expressions from him. He called out "Oh Jesus! I am going to be hung any way, and I will kill all hands before they hang me." I ran downstairs and said, "And who are you going to kill?" He was in an awful rage. I could not tell what was the matter with him. He said he would kill every one of the McCarthys, and I then noticed that his moustache was shaved off. He was clipping away at the doors and plastering, and then ran out of doors and raved and ramped around and said that he was going to kill all hands. He came back again in the evening. He said nothing further about them at that time. He stayed till Sunday morning the 24th. He went away and did not come back again that week — at least I did not see him . . . .
>
> (*The Daily Examiner,* 23 January 1886)

Gillis did not remain distraught. A store keeper, John Haley, found him more self-confident:

> . . . I came into town Monday (25th) and returned on Tuesday. I saw Gillis on that day. He asked what was the news from Charlottetown, and what was going on there.

I saw him again on Wednesday or Thursday. I had heard
of the murder by this time. He said he heard there was a
murder in Charlottetown. I said, yes, I had heard so. I
said I didn't think there was a man on the Island bad
enough to do such a dreadful deed. He said there was
plenty of them in Charlottetown. There were men on the
Boston boat who would do it [Gillis perhaps recalling his
days with the Gloucester fishermen]. He had a hard time
to save himself when he came on the Boston Boat, but
whoever had committed the murder had left the Island
and would never be found out. He said he knew
Callaghan and had driven out to see him. He said those
who robbed him might have left him his life. . . . Callaghan was, he said, a pretty fine old fellow, he thought.
He said he guessed the old fellow had some money — all
Irishmen generally have. I remember when Gillis came
back, it was on a Friday. I met him on the road. He
seemed changed in appearance. His moustache was
shaved off. I asked him what he had been doing to himself. He said he always shaved off in summer because of
the heat. He told me he had been to Charlottetown. He
came into the store and bought a white linen handkerchief. He could have obtained a similar handkerchief in
Charlottetown.

(*The Daily Examiner*, 25 January 1886)

Despite such bravado Gillis' restlessness returned. He soon left
Harmony and returned to Charlottetown, where he used another
pseudonym, that of McCormack. For a time he disappeared in the
woods but reappeared at Harmony, where he was arrested by
Constable McKinnon on June 20th. Aside from Callaghan's watch,
chain and gold piece, there was other incriminating evidence. In
Gillis' trunk, which he had hidden in a field, were found his own
blood-stained clothing as well as a vest, also bloodied, belonging
to the victim. The defence sought to suggest that the latter had been
planted by the real murderer in the trunk while it was in the custody of the police. This argument convinced few.

During much of the trial and sitting through the testimonies of more than forty witnesses, the accused seemed self-possessed, occasionally smiling at the excitement the case generated, but more often sedate. When both the Crown and defence had concluded their cases and the Judge delivered his charge to the Jury, Gillis' composure finally broke. After the Jury had retired, one of the witnesses found himself near the dock. Gillis assailed him: "Damn you, you murdered Callaghan, and why do you stand grinning at me?" Leaning over the dock, the accused tried to strike the witness before being restrained by the Deputy Sheriff and some constables. They handcuffed and took him to the jail. An hour later they brought him back to Court where the Jury returned the verdict of guilty.

Several days later, the Chief Justice sentenced Gillis to be hanged on March 11th, 1886 — the date of his 35th birthday. The condemned man was, however, spared this fate. Shortly before the execution was to occur, the Governor-General executed his prerogative and commuted the sentence to life imprisonment. This was apparently done on the grounds that Gillis had been convicted entirely on the basis of circumstantial evidence. This action did not meet with the approval of all Charlottetowners:

> ... And now the question is asked, why was it done? If at all permissible, it is to be hoped that those who are responsible for the act of the Governor-General will enlighten the public upon the matter. It cannot be that Gillis is considered innocent; if so, he should have been pardoned, and not imprisoned for life. The fact of the sentence being commuted shows that. If there was any doubt about his guilt or innocence, a reprieve, until the matter could have been cleared beyond a doubt, would have been preferable. If a cold-blooded, cruel, merciless crime, such as was proved to have been committed by Gillis, can be perpetrated, and after conviction the sentence of the law be commuted to imprisonment for life, the sooner the death penalty is removed from the Statute Book the better.

There is something repulsive to everyone in the thought of depriving a fellow mortal of his life; but the higher sense of justice which seems implanted in all, for the protection of life and liberty, becomes infinitely more shocked at an evasion of the law than in its being carried out, even in its most sanguinary form.

It is to be hoped that in the interests of the public some explanation may be given, where one is so decidedly needed.

Upton

(*The Daily Examiner,* 9 March 1886)

While at least some questioned the reprieve, the commutation came too late for Gillis' sister and one of the witnesses who testified against him: each became insane after the trial.

In late April Deputy Sheriff Curtis and his assistants delivered the prisoner to Dorchester. On route they were detained at Pictou Landing for several hours. A crowd gathered on the wharf, anxious to get a view of the convicted murderer. After his transfer from the steamer, news that he was on the train spread all along the line. At every station between Pictou and Dorchester the curious sought one last look at the now famous criminal.

In handing over his charge to the warden, Curtis did so with a sense of relief, but also with a warning: "See here! I have had this fellow under my charge for the past year, and all I can say about him is that he needs watching" (*The Daily Examiner,* 24 April 1886). Such perhaps underplayed the community's revulsion for his crime, but aptly suggested how far Gillis was seen to have strayed from the norms of a law-abiding society.

POLICEMAN PARKER'S DEPARTURE

The police themselves were not all equally fit for the battle against "killers, thieves, tramps and sinners," as the case of Moncton's Policeman Parker illustrates. The "guardians" of peace and order in Moncton in the late nineteenth century consisted of the Town Marshal, several other policemen — including those assigned as night policemen — and a small number of constables. Whereas the former were salaried, the latter claimed for such services as the collection of taxes. Although the Marshal was responsible for the daily activities of the Force, the Town Council's Police Committee — consisting of three councilors — had a central role in the monitoring of the guardians' performance. That Committee regularly recommended to Council on the appointment and discharge of individual officers, and investigated any complaints lodged by the citizenry.

To sustain the local justice system, Monctonians were assessed through the 1880s to provide the $600 annual salary of Stipendiary Magistrate Wortman and the $1200 Police account. The Marshal received a monthly salary of $41.67, the other police each claimed approximately $38, although this varied somewhat from month to month. The night policeman was paid $1.25 per night of duty.

As in other Maritime urban communities, town fathers were conscious of this cost. At the November, 1879, meeting of Town Council, Councillor Cowlin moved to dispose of the services of the night policeman by the middle of the month. While he found no fault with the officer, he argued that there was now no need for him and the money might be saved. This action proved immediately shortsighted. The following month, the break-in at A.S. McKay's

Moncton Police, 1894-95 *(Moncton Museum)*

shoe store on Main Street indicated to local merchants the need for the immediate reappointment of a night policeman: "The business men contribute largely to the funds of the town. Many of them have valuable stocks of goods, and they surely are entitled to the protection of an efficient police" (*The Moncton Daily Times*, 31 December 1879).

The Council itself was blamed for not taking effective steps to prevent such a burglary:

... Why should a burglar "fear detection" in Moncton? And haven't almost every species of crime been perpetrated with impunity?

Your correspondent does not lay the blame for this state of things altogether on the one policeman who guards over and protects the interests of the town. One policeman cannot be expected to do duty night and day, though he may be expected to do his duty efficiently.

The Council is to blame for not having an efficient

night policeman on duty. They discharged the late night policeman for the evident reason that his services were not satisfactory. Why did they not say so and try and secure another officer, instead of playing the part of children?

The Council by their action virtually say: We do not believe in the old saying that evil doers love darkness rather than light. We believe that men who contemplate evil will come out on the Main Street, when the sun is brightest and highest, and the biggest crowds are about, to do this nefarious work. This is what the Council virtually say, for do they not have a day policeman and no night watch at all.

Let the Council think the matter over, consider where all the burglaries and other crimes are committed, and then ask themselves if they have not been playing the part of children rather than of men in the matter of police service.

Plain Talk

(The Moncton Daily Times, 31 December 1879)

Ironically, as if to prove the critics wrong, Marshal Steadman immediately arrested one Thomas Warren for the burglary at the McKay store. Perhaps suspicious that he had been the first person to inform the Marshal of the break-in, Steadman indicated he had kept "his eye" on Warren all day, ascertaining where he had spent a silver dollar which was missing after the break-in. Warren admitted his guilt.

Such quick action did not mute fears of continued property crime. Soon thereafter the Police Committee returned a night policeman to Moncton's streets. In January, 1880, Jason Cormair was assigned night duty as a "special" for a brief time. He was replaced by Edward Parker. Asking for an advance in pay which Council refused to do, however, Parker's tenure was also abbreviated. He was able to return as night policeman the following July when his demands were met, receiving $30 a month as salary.

It was soon evident that Parker was not the best of "guardians." In late September he was faulted for not ensuring the streets were peaceful:

Is there any person within the limits of our Corporation who can inform a reader of the *Times* where the great Parker ("Policeman"), Lawyer and Judge of "Editorial manhood" was last night when a quarto of drunken roughs were alarming the citizens and arousing the virtuous from their pleasant dreams, and causing the Proprietor of the Phoenix Hotel to exclaim in vain, "where, oh where, is Parker? Where, oh where, can *he* be?"

He (Parker) was searched for but could not be found. These night prowlers, when last seen, were making their way to the Railroad Station, but they had better been conducted to the [Police] Station at the lower end of town. It is yet a mystery where Mr. Parker could be but probably he was in a fit of *serious reflection* over his last brutal assault.

I would like for Mr. Parker to inform the citizens of Moncton, whose servant he is supposed to be, why he shirked his duty on Tuesday night; and why he did not arrest the party above referred to, as well as he did Mr. John Gillespie, who from all accounts was minding his own business when he was snatched and pummelled and locked up like a dumb animal.

(*The Moncton Daily Times,* 23 September 1880)

Parker's failings also apparently included a proclivity toward excessive use of force. This was evident during the testimony heard before Magistrate Wortman regarding the policeman's arrest of John Gillespie on a charge of being drunk and disorderly.

THE PARKER-GILLESPIE CASE

Policeman Parker charged John Gillespie with being drunk and disorderly and with assaulting him while in the discharge of his duty. The prisoner had been arrested at an early hour Sunday morning.

Gillespie was unable to attend Court on Monday because of injuries to his head he had received during the arrest. The case was subsequently heard.

Edward Parker: Am Policeman, Town of Moncton. About 1 or 2 o'clock Sunday morning last, was going up Main street and on passing the foot of Vulcan street noticed a man coming down that street. By his walk I thought he was under the influence of liquor. I took particular notice to see if I knew the man, but I did not. He turned up Main street, but did not go far till he turned about and walked back. Saw he was a stranger to me and then went over and spoke to the man. Asked him which way he was going. He said he was going to the Central House. I said, "You are travelling down street, instead of up — do you know which way you are going?" He said, "Damn you, do you think I am a damned fool?" I then arrested him. He asked me what I arrested him for — said he was not drunk, and had only two glasses. He also said we will go along and talk it over. We got down near the corner of the Bank (say 200 feet) when he turned around and struck me on the left cheek. I struck back with the billy. He then struck me again on the right side of the nose. I struck him again and he struck me in the breast. The last place I struck him was on the right side of the head. He fell, then, with me on top, and I took him to the lock-up.

Cross-examined: I took no liquor that night. Took some one morning in the Phoenix. In the winter I took liquor once or twice. This night (the night of Gillespie's arrest) was a fine moonlight night. Johnson Parker was with us on the night in question. He was with me all the time up to three o'clock, and was with me when I saw Gillespie. Gillespie was not noisy or disorderly until after I spoke to him. The reason I accosted him was that I thought he was a stranger, so did not know his way to his hotel, and I felt it my duty to direct him. I smelt liquor on him. He walked crooked. I don't know that I saw him stagger. I think I struck him four times with my baton. I strike moderately. My son was standing across the street by McSweeney's building when this took place. I did not call him to assist me. My son assisted me with the handcuffs. Gillespie walked handcuffed to lockup. At the time I first struck him I was at the first corner of Bank. I noticed the blood on the spot, probably the next day. I did not use my fist on prisoner. I think he called for a doctor after I put handcuffs on him. I don't think he said he was bleeding to death. He asked me to put my finger in the cuts. I did not say, "damn you I will give you another blow." I will not swear that he did or did not say he would die if I did not take him to a doctor. He asked me in cell to bring a doctor or take him to one. I did neither. Don't know when his wounds were dressed, but they were not as long as I had charge of him, which was till 5 in the morning. I saw more than one wound in his head — saw two. Did not examine closely. Felt the cut on forehead in cell, when he asked me to. I am told Gillespie has lived in town for six years. Did not know him. I don't know anything about the man's respectability. He was a stranger to me. (Baton used shown in Court.) When he asked me what I arrested him for I told him for drunkenness. I often see people on street at night drunker than Gillespie was, and do not arrest them but go home with them. Gillespie said he wasn't about to get up when I put handcuffs on him. Did not drag him across street. When Gillespie asked me to take him to a doctor I told him he was all right. He asked me to go to D.A. Duffy with him and get bail. I did not. He asked me to go to P. McSweeney. I told him Mr. McSweeney was in Ottawa. I am not in the habit of releasing prisoners on bail. Think I remember of releasing one prisoner, but am not positive.

Re-examined: Have been on duty over two months this last term. Always carry a baton, and think it is my privilege to use it if a prisoner shows fight. I make as many arrests at or near Vulcan street as in any other part of town. When people behave I do not arrest them. If prisoner had not replied as he did I would not have arrested him, but would have followed him home.

Gillespie did not say at the time I accosted him that he was waiting for a friend.

Johnson Parker: Was on street with my father the morning Gillespie was arrested. Left police office, went up town and when opposite Mrs. Dowd's bar, noticed a man coming down Vulcan street near the foot. When he got to the foot, he turned to his right and went as far as upper corner of Gunnin's harness shop. Returned and was walking down street slowly, when policeman Parker started across the street and said something to him. Did not hear what Gillespie said. They then walked down street as far as corner of bank, policeman Parker having hold of Gillespie's coat collar. When they got to corner of Bank accused made a sudden jump and struck at policeman Parker. He struck back. Do not know how many times they struck. They went to the ground together. Parker took out his handcuffs and put one on Gillespie's left wrist; gave me the key to unlock the other. I did so. Before he got the second handcuff on accused tried to get up, but did not. Parker took another instrument from his pocket and put it on the right wrist. Gillespie then got up and was taken to the police station.

Cross-examined: Did not take handcuffs off immediately putting him in the cell; about ten minutes after. He asked for a doctor; also asked for bonds for his appearance; also asked for water, and asked to get out. He asked for Mr. Duffy and Mr. Delahunt. Mr. Parker gave him water to wash his head. Can't recollect Mr. Parker refusing to give him water. Was out till 3 o'clock. Was on duty with Parker till that hour. Could have heard any conversation that passed between them. Saw Mr. Gillespie stumble at foot of Vulcan street, but didn't see him fall down. Didn't see him acting drunk, disorderly or talking loud. Couldn't swear whether he was up Vulcan street 50 yards or not. Think he was this side of Mr. Cameron's house. Won't swear Parker had him by arm or not. Don't know whether he struck Parker or not. Parker struck Gillespie and drew blood; struck him more than once; don't know how often. Was about 10 or 15 feet from where Parker struck Gillespie. Wasn't taking particular notice of the striking. Saw blood on ground and on Mr. Gillespie's face. Both fell to the ground. They were clinched and Parker knocked him down. I don't recollect hearing him ask for a doctor while at Bank corner. Said he would die if left in lockup this morning. At the request of Parker I helped to take Gillespie to the lockup. Gillespie asked me to take hold of his arm; that he was weak — very weak; took hold of arm. Asked Gillespie while going down to the lockup not to shake the blood on his (witness') clothes. After falling down he was helped up. Told Gillespie he had better go down quiet as he might cut up worse than he had been. Came out with my father that night with my own accord. Swear Gillespie wasn't dragged on the ground. Don't remember seeing Mr. Gillespie try to get up and fall on the ground again. Before handcuff was put on Mr. Gillespie didn't try to get up. Walked with him to lockup, and don't recollect his asking for Mr. Duffy. Mr. Gillespie told me who he was, and where he stopped. Didn't hear him tell father that he was waiting for anyone. Did not see any person around that night. Heard Gillespie say that he was not drunk.

H.A. Whitney (sworn): Am Mechanical Superintendent I.C.R. Am acquainted with Mr. Gillespie; he is a machinist and fitter; has been in the service 5 or 6 years. His character to sobriety and faithfulness is good. Foreman always spoke well of him, as a steady, sober man. Haven't known him to lose an hour's work for any misconduct whatsoever. Won't swear whether he was ever drunk while in Moncton, but he always attended his work.

Geo. P. Thomas (sworn): Was in Miss Walton's oyster saloon on Telegraph Street, between 1 and 2 Sunday morning. Went for refreshments. Was sitting in front room waiting for oyster stew. Did not drink any liquor there. Had not drank any liquor for several days before, nor since. Heard noise on street apparently out in front of the Bank on Main Street. Saw three men together; they were talking quite lively. Heard one man say, "Parker, what did you arrest me for, for I am sober." Heard Parker say, "Yes, but you gave me impudence." I then saw some struggling, and both fell to the ground. There seemed to be a lull for a time; after a moment I heard this man say, "For God's sake take me to a doctor." Parker says, "I'll take you to the lockup." The man said, "For God's sake don't take me there. I'll die before morning." In the meantime, saw two men standing away from man that was lying down, and Parker said, "Come, get up and come along." He made three unsuccessful attempts to get up, and each time fell back. The man the voice came from was crying, "Take me to a doctor, quick." Am of the impression Parker took him by the hands and dragged him across street. Have since inspected the spot — about 10 or 11 same day, and found pool of blood, also found a stick there saturated with blood. When I saw Mr. G. he was lying on bed, with sticking plaster on his head and face swelled tolerably. If I had a dog in the same condition, would shoot him to put him out of misery.

Cross-examined: There were several gentlemen in Miss Walton's with me — say three; were talking and chatting. Had nothing there except oysters. When I heard noise up Telegraph Street, looked out window, for say three minutes. We were not holding a prayer meeting in the house at the time. The noise was out on the street this side of bank. Swear I heard every word while I had my head out of window. It occurred just as detailed by me. I said to the rest inside that Parker was taking someone to lockup. I think I would run if I heard anybody cry help or murder. Will swear positively that I saw the man try three unsuccessful attempts to get up, but don't know whether it was Gillespie or not. His feet were toward Mr. Duff's building and head toward the westward. The other two men were standing by. Could see everything very plain from where I was. No one besides myself looking out the window. Was in about half an hour or so.

Mrs. Dowd (sworn): Recollect last Sabbath morning. There was a loud noise, and cries of a man, on Main Street. Was in bed, and window was up; looked out and listened for a while, and the noise appeared to be getting louder. Went through to front part of house and looked out of window, but could see no person. Went out back door, through to Main street and sidewalk, in front of McSweeney's building. Saw three men on street toward McS.'s building. One of the men was down. Mr. Parker was one of them, but didn't know the other two. The man that was down made an attempt to get up, and fell down again. He said, "Oh, God, don't drag me; I'm not in a condition to be dragged." The man apparently in front of him had him by the hands, pulling him up, but he fell down again. He said not to take him any farther, that his head was all cut. Parker said he'd get a doctor for him, and I think swore an oath at the time. The third attempt the other man took hold of him and hauled him up. There was no person to be seen up or down the street, nowhere. The man said he was under the doctor's hands, and was not fit to be dragged about. Think the man was pretty badly injured. He appeared to be sober. They were dragging him along and he cried to them to stop.

Ed. Daley (sworn): Have been acquainted with Mr. Gillespie the last 22 years. Never knew him intoxicated in his life.

D. A. Duffy (sworn): Know Mr. Gillespie. He has had a good character, and all acquainted with him know him as such.

John Dowd (sworn): Recollect last Saturday night. Saw Mr. Gillespie between 12 and 1 o'clock. He was perfectly sober, and would not expect to find him in any other condition. When we parted, he said, "Good night, John," and I bid him the time of night also.

Based on the testimony presented the Magistrate dismissed the charges against the accused (The Moncton Daily Times, 25 September 1880).

When Parker's additional charge of assault against Gillespie while in the discharge of his duty was dismissed, along with that of being drunk and disorderly, the Police Committee immediately recommended the night policeman's suspension. A special meeting of Town Council was held to consider the matter. Several of the councillors argued that the Committee's report should have been more explicit — in particular, indicating whether Parker should be dismissed, or if suspended, for what length of time and for what reason. Councillor Babang explained "that the report was arrived in consequence of the decision of the Court in Mr. Gillespie's case, but as chairman of the Committee he had thought it would be sufficient to recommend suspension, which might be for an indefinite length of time. The other members of the Committee also agreed to that view of the matter while in committee" (*The Moncton Daily Times,* 29 September 1880). This was not good enough for Council; the Committee changed its recommendation to one of dismissal, which was adopted. Ferdinand Thibideau was appointed as Parker's replacement, at least initially on a temporary basis.

The matter did not end there. In a short time Council received a petition from "some forty odd leading citizens and ratepayers" asking for Parker's reinstatement (*The Moncton Daily Times,* 16 October 1880). An October meeting of Council saw some rather unusual maneuvering:

> ... On the consideration of the petition coming up, a motion was made for the reinstatement of Parker, an amendment asked for the permanent appointment of Thibideau, and an amendment to the amendment was to the effect that the petition be referred to the Police Committee. The amendment to the amendment passed by a vote of three to one, Coun. Babang voting for it, though he spoke against it. It is fair to say, that Coun. Babang had a motive in voting in favor of something he was opposed to, his object probably being to prevent a vote on the first amendment, which asked for the permanent employment of Mr. Thibideau as night policeman . . . .
>
> (*The Moncton Daily Times,* 25 September 1880)

The referral of the issue back to the Police Committee was unnecessary. Within the week Parker indicated that he would not accept reinstatement, even if it were offered. The guardian had departed.

THE MURDER OF
POLICEMAN STEADMAN

Tragedy struck Moncton's police force in dramatic fashion. One Friday night in late July, 1892, W. Wilson & Co.'s store at Chatham was burglarized. The safe was blown open and approximately $250 in cash and silver taken. Word of the theft reached Moncton quickly. Attention quickly focused on two suspicious-looking men, known as Buck and Jim, who had reached Moncton Saturday night. They had taken lodging at Mrs. Donnelly's rather notorious house on Telegraph Street, not far from the Park Hotel. Moncton's Police Marshal Foster telegraphed Chatham to confirm the description of those suspected of the burglary and of the kind of money taken (which included Mexican silver coins). Foster initially intended to arrest the two suspects early in the evening, but delayed until he was certain they were present at the Donnelly house. The Marshal advised night policeman Scott, "We've got an ugly job on hand tonight." Joseph Steadman, also a night policeman, special constable Charles Colborne, and a citizen named Alexander McRae were enlisted for the raid. Foster later recalled Steadman's fateful advice as they prepared for the raid: "On the way up Joe asked me how I was going to manage it. I said I was going in the front door. He said: If you do you will never come out alive" (*The Moncton Daily Times*, 2 August 1892).

Sending Steadman to the side door and Scott and Colborne to the back, Foster entered the Donnelly house with a baton in one hand and a revolver in the other. Inside at the time were Mrs. Donnelly, her two daughters, Maggie and Selina, a son, Thomas, Ira Germain and John Dryden. On seeing Foster, Selina gave the alarm: "Foster is here." Buck pulled out a revolver and yelled to his companion, "Hi Jim." Both rushed for the side door. While Jim escaped, Buck ran into Steadman and a struggle ensued. Shots were fired. Constable Scott hearing the shooting ran to where Steadman had been, and saw him grappling with Buck. Scott helped subdue the latter. Steadman released his hold, staggered a few steps, exclaiming "My God, boys, I'm shot," and collapsed. He was immediately carried to the sitting room of the Park Hotel, where it was confirmed that he was dead. In handcuffs Buck was taken to the lockup, begging Scott for relief from further blows:

"My God, don't hit me again, my head is broken."

"You didn't get half enough."

"I did not do it."

(*The Moncton Daily Times,* 3 August 1892)

After his arrest Buck — described as about 30, 5' 7", 150 lbs, with high cheek bones, small eyes, "brutish and rough looking," and unshaven for several weeks — refused to give his name. When efforts later were made to photograph him, he deliberately covered his face. Though denying he did the shooting, the bullet which remained in his leg was a painful reminder of this encounter with the "long arm of the law."

Buck's denial was vacuous. A Smith and Wesson revolver was immediately retrieved in the yard where the scuffle with Steadman had taken place. Two of its five chambers were empty; none of the officers' revolvers had been discharged. Buck's coat, as additional evidence, was found marked with powder.

After Steadman had been carried to the Park Hotel, a crowd gathered and remained through the night, periodically urging that the culprit now in custody be lynched. Two constables were assigned to guard the lockup. Especially evocative of the tragedy of the night, the slain officer's dog, which often accompanied him on his beat, wandered up and down the street. Finally catching the scent of his master at the Park Hotel, the bewildered animal tried to enter the room where the body was laid out.

An inquest was quickly arranged the next day in Moncton's Police Court. Marshal Foster and the other participants in the night's events, as well as several witnesses, all recounted what they had seen of the confrontation between Buck and Steadman. The jury without much deliberation concluded

> that on the evening of the first day of August inst., the said Jos. E. Steadman while in discharge of his duty as such police officer attempting to make an arrest of two persons who were stopping at the house on Telegraph Street in the said city of Moncton, known as the Donnelly house, suspected of breaking a safe at Chatham, belonging to Wilson & Co., and taking therefrom a sum of money, he came to his death by a shot fired from a revolver in the hands of a person to us unknown, and called "Buck", who is now in custody and that he fired the said shot with intent to kill and murder the said Joseph E. Steadman.

> (*The Moncton Daily Times,* 3 August 1892)

City Council urged a speedy trial of Buck. The Police Committee resolved to offer a reward of $250 for the apprehension of his confederate. Both actions reflected not only horror at the killing of one of their guardians. Buck and Jim were suspected of being members of a gang of tramps and burglars who had recently infested the provinces; Moncton's citizenry could not tolerate such depredations.

As Buck awaited his fate behind bars, the search for Jim extended throughout the surrounding countryside. Constables were dispatched wherever his presence was supposedly discovered. A farmer wandering the fields looking for his cows was released after his identity was clarified; another in Sussex was able to convince authorities he was not the fugitive they sought. He had only come to town to prepare for his wedding — which accounted for a clean shave, new suit of clothes and "mysterious actions." Reports were received from Salisbury and from Port Elgin that Jim had finally been captured. But these proved illusory. Buck was affected by the frenetic search, frequently querying his captors if Jim had yet been arrested. Expressing some panic, the prisoner told the Marshal he would tell everything if his own life could be spared. Admitting that there were five in his gang, he still refused to give his name. The first official confirmation of his identity, however, came in a telegram received from one Detective Gross of Montreal, who identified Buck as Buck Whelan, "well known in Montreal as a very desperate character." With his companion, Jim Christie, he was alleged to have burglarized the Sackville post office as well as establishments in other communities.

As the search for Jim continued — now spurred on by an additional reward offered of $500 — Buck was brought before Moncton's Stipendiary Wortman for preliminary examination. The prisoner now seemed less reluctant to identify himself. He claimed his name was Robert Olsen, a Norwegian by birth, whose parents had emigrated to America twenty years previously, settling on a farm outside St. Paul, Minnesota. To Thomas Donnelly hours before the shooting he had claimed to be a sailor off a schooner at Saint John. When Donnelly asked where he was going, the response was "it's none of your business." Buck insisted he had only been in Moncton twice, but vigorously denied Moncton's ex-Marshal Thibideau's accusation that he was the individual that police officer had attempted to capture four years earlier for the Dorchester post office burglary.

Public feeling against the prisoner continued unabated. Crowds gathered on Main Street discussing the case. Several hundred Monctonians loitered around the police station. Passions ran high as the largest funeral procession ever seen in Moncton assembled to lay the slain constable to rest. The body was enclosed in a casket borne by members of the Orange Order. The widow and now fatherless son may have taken solace from the various eulogies:

> In the death of policeman Steadman, Moncton has lost a faithful officer and man who, with all his failings — and who is without them — had many friends. But in the performance of his duty the dead officer has no favorites .... As an officer he was fearless and bold in doing his duty, and his affable manner in the performance of such won for him many friends ....
>
> (*The Moncton Daily Times,* 6 August 1892)

Perhaps too affable. A native of Moncton, Steadman had actually served as Moncton's first Police Marshal after the town's incorporation. Eight years earlier, in January 1884, Steadman was suspended from the force for three months, with Policeman Thibideau promoted to serve as his replacement. At the end of his period of suspension, Town Council by a very close vote reinstated Steadman. One month later — again by a close margin, with the Mayor casting the deciding vote — this was reversed and Thibideau was permanently appointed Marshal. The winter of 1884, indeed, had been marked by considerable turmoil in Moncton's police circles. In late February, the Police Magistrate had sought unsuccessfully to dismiss all of Moncton's policemen and constables for not enforcing the Scott Act. Presumably the failure to deal vigorously enough with liquor violations had also prompted Steadman's suspension. In any case, although no longer Marshal, Steadman subsequently gained employment as a night policeman, in which capacity he ultimately met his tragic end. His murder elicited considerable interest throughout the Maritimes (where this incident was one more reminder of the outgrowth of the tramp nuisance and the need to control their propensity for burglary) and elsewhere. The *Montreal Gazette* observed how this incident underscored the importance of local "guardians":

> The killing of Constable Steadman at Moncton is another reminder that the policeman's lot is not a happy one. Canada is happily comparatively free from affairs of this kind, though they occur with a frequency that lets people know how useful the blue coat and baton are, and how serious is the work their wearers are engaged in.
>
> (*The Montreal Gazette,* 5 August 1892)

Eulogies, lessons, public forms of commiseration did not distract Monctonians from the more immediate quest to deal convincingly with the culprits of this tragedy. The preliminary examination of Buck quickly concluded and he was committed to trial at Dorchester, still pleading not guilty. The police continued to receive numerous reports of Jim's whereabouts. It was speculated that he had not travelled far. A cow at Salisbury emerged from the woods milked dry. The rumour that he had returned to the Donnelly house excited a rush of the citizenry there without success. That the fugitive remained at large was a source of considerable alarm to many:

> About 11 o'clock last night a man went to the door of Mr. Geo. Willett's house on Fleet street and demanded admittance. Mr. Willett was at the Telegraph office and Mrs. Willett was alone with the children when she heard three pretty loud raps at the door. On asking who was there she was greeted with the answer that it was a "gentleman." Mrs. Willett was not satisfied with such an answer and demanded to know what was wanted. The miscreant failed to give a satisfactory answer and Mrs. Willett aroused the neighbours next door, when the man skipped.
>
> (*The Moncton Daily Times*, 5 August 1892)

Despite a number of false sightings, it was not until the 11th of August that Jim was finally captured at Bass River by Pictou's detective Peter O. Carroll. After Jim was safely deposited in the lockup, the Police Committee permitted a number of the citizenry to view the prisoner. As had occurred with Buck, speculation focused on Jim's real identity: "Judging from his talk, Jim has doubtless been well educated and appears to be pretty well read on matters in general." Claiming to be from Toronto, Jim boasted that he had "always been used to city life."

Buck and Jim were both taken to the County Jail at Dorchester where they were tried at the Circuit Court. After the grand jurors had been duly sworn, Judge Fraser summarized the facts of the case. With these presented before them, he did not believe the jury would have any difficulty in concluding that Steadman had come to his death at the hands of Buck. The Judge acknowledged the question could arise whether the assailant actually knew that Steadman was a police officer. He thought it reasonable to assume that he did, especially in light of the evidence that the "guardian" had been pointed out to both Buck and Jim on the street before that eventful night. After deliberating almost three hours, the Grand Jury brought in a true bill for murder against Buck and indicted

Jim on seven counts — including discharging a pistol at Steadman, feloniously, wilfully and with malice. Both prisoners pleaded not guilty. Attorney-General Blair moved for trial. Foster, addressing Buck, asked "Are you ready for trial?" Without hesitation and in a loud tone came the response: "About as ready as I can ever get." Each prisoner had a different counsel, and was to be tried separately. R.B. Smith was engaged to defend Jim by a "strange rough talking man," who, it was alleged, had secured the necessary funds from "the fraternity of tramps in the upper provinces."

Buck's trial began slowly, as considerable time was given to selection of the jury. Thirty possible candidates were examined. Defence especially objected to those who were members of the Orange Order, fearing that they would be strongly biased against their slain brother's attacker. After the jury had been chosen, the Sheriff announced that one of the jurymen had been taken ill. Unable to proceed with the trial, the Attorney-General moved that the jury be discharged. The Judge agreed. A new empaneling process commenced. Finally the case was heard, with the Attorney-General serving as the prosecution. Much of the testimony from witnesses and others repeated what had been heard previously. Yet something new was added. An especially damning piece of evidence was the conversation between Buck and Jim which Detective Carroll overheard after he had apprehended the latter and stayed the night in the same jail as the prisoners:

Q. — Did you subsequently come to Dorchester and while here were the prisoners in confinement?

A. — Yes, sir.

Q. — Were you in the jail and did you hear any conversation?

A. — Yes, sir; on the night of August 16.

Q. — You knew the room in which they were confined?

A. — I did.

Q. — How many were they situated?

A. — There was one cell between the two.

Q. — Where were you?

A. — In the cell alongside of Jim.

Q. — Did you hear them talking to one another?

A. — Yes, sir.

Q. — You distinguished their voices?

A. — Yes, sir; I knew which was Jim and which was Buck. They commenced to talk about 2 o'clock.

Q. — How long had you been there before that?

A. — I remained there from 9 o'clock. The conversation took place on the morning of August 17th. Jim got up and sung out, "Olsen, Olsen." Jim said: "Hi, Olsen, is that you?" Olsen says: "Yes; is that you, Jim?" Jim answered: "Yes, everything is quiet."

Jim said: "I had a hard time since I saw you last."

Olsen said: "Yes, and I had a hard time of it since I saw you last."

Jim said: "We will have to take our chances. You made a h__l of a job of it."

Buck said: "Perhaps you would have done the same if you were in my place. When I fired that shot I thought I would get clear, but the other policeman knocked me stiff with a club."

Jim said: "There's only one thing we can do now."

Buck said: "What's that, Jim?"

Jim said: "We will have to take our chances."

Olsen said: "Your chances are all right, Jim."

Jim said: "It's a pity I didn't fix the big fellow [i.e., Carroll] but he was too quick for me."

Olsen said: "He gave you a pretty good smashing up."

Jim said, "Yes."

(The Moncton Daily Times, 17 September 1892)

As Carroll recounted this exchange, Buck reacted with derision from the defendant's box. Defence cross-examined the Pictou detective, focusing particularly on whether his witness to this conversation might have been clouded by too many drinks that night. Carroll admitted to three or four drinks of sherry but nothing more.

William Wilson arrived from Chatham to identify the silver

coins taken from Buck at the time of his arrest. As they had done repeatedly, others took the stand to describe what they had witnessed the night of the shooting. D. Grant, Buck's counsel, addressed the jury in a 2½ hour summation, arguing that Buck had been arrested without a warrant (which was true), and that therefore he had the right to resist an unlawful arrest. By this logic, Grant pointed out, the charge should have been that of manslaughter, not that of murder. Counsel sought to raise doubts in the minds of the jurors. Why had the Crown not insisted that the bullet still in Buck's leg be removed? Was it because it might not have come from either Buck's or Jim's revolver but rather from one of those in the arresting party? Could it not have been the case that Steadman's billy club actually struck the trigger of his revolver, resulting in an accidental shooting?

In his rebuttal, Attorney-General Blair would have none of Grant's reasoning:

> . . . These officers did not go there with warrants. They went there as the law shows. They were making an arrest on reasonable suspicion. There is that in the law that requires warrants to be got, but it is their duty to go in many cases without warrants under many circumstances. In this one it seems to me, it was their duty to go, for it will be remembered that the names of the parties were not known and to this day one of them is not known yet. It would be a little difficult to get out warrants for them in this case. I think we have shown you that these officers went there to make this arrest on very reasonable suspicions, that these persons might reasonably be suspected of this crime [of burglary in Chatham]. We have these people properly under suspicion and we have an officer going there properly to effect their arrest, I do not know any other way a careful officer would start to work to arrest such desperate men as these men proved themselves to be. What other course could they take but to surround the house? The officers are not called upon to handle such people as these with gloves but to set to

work with all reasonable hazards to effect their arrest on information. It is the business of the officers to stop them from roaming around the country when they reasonably suspect them of crime. When a person is being arrested without a warrant it is the duty of the officer to make known, or be reasonably satisfied that the person he is arresting has some knowledge that he is arresting him. Any notice that conveys to the mind of the man that his arrest is about to be procured is all that the law requires. It appears to me His Honour will tell you that if the statement made were true there was sufficient notice that the prisoner was being arrested. He knew the officers were upon him and if he knew this what more notice could he have. The law does not require any more. We have the fact that these people committed the crime, that they were in the house, which at all events was not of the very highest reputation. About 9 o'clock an officer of the law entered the house and on that moment the prisoner is notified and when you have got the fact that he knew that an account of the Chatham burglary was in the morning paper, it is clear he had notice enough that he was about to be arrested. He had been about 2 or 3 days and I think it may be reasonabl[y] supposed he had made himself acquainted as to who the officers were and when he heard the warning that Selina Donnelly gave he would know what it meant and make his escape. I think you will have reasonable grounds to suppose from all these circumstances that he had sufficient notice that the officers were there to effect his arrest, and for no other purpose. Therefore it seems to me that you will find it difficult in saying anything else than that when the prisoner jumped from the table and rushed from that room he did so with the knowledge that these were officers. You have got to believe that he either knew it was an officer whom he met or that it was some one trying to commit a crime upon him. Which is the most reasonable theory? Did the prisoner not know when he was confronted by Steadman that he was confronted by an officer who was effecting his arrest? Whatever else happened the man who was seeking to make the arrest lost his life while in defence of the peace. If the prisoner did it there is only one conclusion you can arrive at and that is that the prisoner is guilty of the crime with which he is charged, that is murder . . . .

(*The Moncton Daily Times,* 19 September 1892)

Without extended deliberation the jury agreed. Sentence was reserved until after Jim's trial had been completed. As with that of his confederate, many of the same witnesses were called to testify as had been heard earlier. Corroborating what Carroll had said, a young boy named Henry James was brought forward to report on a conversation he had overheard between Buck and Jim. James had been serving a short sentence and was working about the jail:

. . . Jones says that on Tuesday morning, Aug. 23rd, while going to sweep out the hall running along at the head of the corridors in which the cells are, he heard the prisoners, Buck and Jim, talking about the shooting at Moncton. The hall, he says, was covered with mats, so any one could not easily be heard. Jones says he was going out of the kitchen hall to sweep the corridor when he heard Buck say to Jim, "My God, I am sorry I shot him now. I almost cried after I heard the people say how good a man he was, but I could not help it. I went to point the revolver to fire and in doing so some one hit me on the head which made me drop my revolver quite a piece. I intended to raise my revolver again, to shoot over his shoulder but I got another clout over the head that made me drop my revolver just as I was going to pull the trigger." Buck said he was sorry he did not point the revolver at Foster when he first saw him . . . .

(*The Moncton Daily Times,* 20 September 1892)

Court was also advised that Jim was to be arraigned on another charge — that of burglary of J.B. Miller's store at Molus River.

This apparently had occurred several nights after the shooting of Steadman, while Jim was seeking to elude his pursuers.

Detective Carroll returned to the stand and recounted how he had apprehended Jim. On their return to Moncton, despite the officer's warning that anything he now said could be used against him, Jim admitted to having fired four shots on the night of the murder and was terribly frightened that he, not Buck, had actually shot Steadman. When Carroll told him a No. 32 cartridge, which matched Buck's revolver, had been found in the deceased, he expressed relief: "Thank God I didn't shoot him. God help Buck."

Opening for the defence, Smith admitted that Jim was a "bad man" but could not be found guilty under the present indictment. The most noteworthy witness called to substantiate this was Buck himself. Identifying himself as Robert Olsen, he claimed to be "paralyzed drunk" the night of the shooting. He said that he and Jim had been expecting a third party to arrive on the train that night. This rather mysterious accomplice had been in the yard when the encounter with Steadman had occurred. Buck's testimony abruptly ended when he refused to tell where he had been before his ill-fated stay in Moncton.

The jury was not swayed by Buck's testimony. Jim was found guilty of four of the seven counts — including that of intent to wound Steadman — but not of murder. The Judge was now ready for the sentencing of the two prisoners. He showed little sympathy toward Jim: "Prisoner at the bar, you are yet a young man but from all we can learn your career has been one of crime . . . you are one of a band of robbers, burglars, and murderers who are travelling throughout the length and breadth of this land committing crimes" (*The Moncton Daily Times,* 23 September 1892). Allowed to make a final statement, Jim suggested that Buck's "third party" was actually responsible for the shooting. This was not persuasive. Jim was sentenced to 25 years in Dorchester. His partner was to have a more irrevocable fate. Rejecting the defence's plea for a new trial in the Supreme Court, the Judge served Buck over to be hanged on December 1st, 1892.

Preparations were immediately begun for the execution. An

annex to the jail was constructed — a wall 18 by 22 feet and 20 feet high, that would ensure, in accordance with the law regarding such events, that Buck's end was shielded from the "vulgar gaze" of the public. The hangman, Radcliffe of Toronto, who apparently had experience with such matters in Ontario, oversaw the instrument of death:

> The gallows consisted of two upright posts about eight feet; apart upon these posts rest[ed] a cross beam. Attached to this beam were two pulleys, one in the centre which received the rope attached to Buck's neck. The rope was run through a second pulley on the outside of one of the posts and fastened up to the iron weight of 346 pounds. The weight was held up to the beam by a trip hook, and by means of this trip hook the weight was dropped.
>
> (*The Moncton Daily Times,* 1 December 1892)

Radcliffe assured all that by jerking the condemned prisoner into the air the end would be more humane than if the more primitive drop method was used.

Buck showed little interest in these preparations. While he was eating his last dinner rather heartily, he received a visit from Shediac's Councillor Russell. Advised there was no hope of a reprieve, Buck responded, "No, I have been told there is none, but perhaps it is all for the best. I believe if I had got clear it might have been worse for me in the future. Nobody can tell. I intend to die like a man if I have to go." Such bravado, however, may have yielded somewhat as Father Cormier, who had been charged with ministering to Buck's spiritual needs in these last hours, brought the prisoner a letter from his accomplice:

> Dorchester Pen'y. Nov. 30, 1892.
>
> Dear Friend — I am sincerely sorry you must die, old friend. It is some consolation to know that you have devoted the last days of your life in preparing your mind to meet God. No one can sympathize more sincerely with you than I have. I would have done anything in my power to save your life but I am as powerless to aid you as you

are to help yourself. We both owe a debt of gratitude to your spiritual advisor for his earnest effort to save not only your life but your soul. It is never too late for God's forgiveness Buck, if we ask His forgiveness with a repentant heart. Forget the world and fix your heart on eternity. Ask God's forgiveness for the sake of that Saviour who died for us all. A few years and we all must appear before our Maker to answer for our deeds. I wish I could shake your hand once more, but if I never do, it will be a source of satisfaction the rest of my life to know you died like a good Christian. Once [more] I urge you to earnestly seek God's forgiveness. Good bye, old friend; may we both one day meet our Saviour in Paradise and be satisfied in His presence. May God please to take you to himself is the fervent prayer of your old friend.

Jim

(The Moncton Daily Times, 1 December 1892)

Whether the spiritual advisor himself shaped the contents of this letter is unknown. This was not to be the last communication between the two prisoners. The evening before the hanging, Dorchester's Warden Foster and guards brought Jim to bid farewell to Buck in person. They talked for some time. Jim asked if he wanted some tobacco. Buck replied, "No, I have enough to last me through." The partners discussed their trials and the evidence that had been brought forward. They agreed that perhaps their capture and conviction had been for the best as they might have come to an even worse end. Their parting was an emotional one:

Jim: "Good bye, old fellow, bear up."

Buck: "Take care of yourself up there."

Jim was one among several visitors Buck received in the waning hours. Representatives of the Women's Christian Temperance Union appeared and sang several hymns for the benefit of the doomed prisoner. On a less spiritual level, a police inspector from Boston, one C.M. Hanscom, arrived to interview Buck, as well as Jim, regarding their possible involvement in the robbery of the Vanderbilts' cottage at Bar Harbor. Although unsuccessful in obtaining any admission of guilty, Hanscom was convinced that both were professional burglars, who had employed numerous aliases, and "only travelled around in tough looking rigs to convey the impression they were ordinary tramps." Noticing a small mend at the bottom of Buck's hip pocket allegedly caused by the constant wearing of a pistol, the inspector expressed no doubt that the two pursued their wide-spread victimization fully armed. Little sympathy for the condemned man was also expressed by Radcliffe, the hangman. Ensconced in the sitting room of a local hotel, he spoke lightly of the next day's execution. Admitting, however, that he did not really like the job, he wished he were a thousand miles away with his wife and "little ones."

Buck slept fairly soundly his last night, although he did complain once or twice of pain in his back. He awoke at 7 a.m. without being called. He was to have only 2½ more hours of life.

7:30 a.m. — Father Cormier holds a religious service for the condemned man. He cannot administer extreme unction; this sacrament can only be given to those in danger of death from natural causes.

8:00 a.m. — Mrs. Atkinson of the W.C.T.U. visits Buck, who gives no sign of breaking down.

9:00 a.m. — Buck appears in the corridor, smiles at the few assembled. Among those present is Judge Landry, who believes Buck "has extraordinary nerve and is the coolest man of the party." Minutes before, he receives an unsigned telegram urging him to ask forgiveness and prepare for death. Buck asks the Sheriff to raise the window so that he can look over to the penitentiary where Jim is housed. The fog obscures his view. There is to be no commutation of sentence despite Jim's alleged confession that he, not Buck, fired the fatal shot.

9:30 a.m. — A procession including the Sheriff, Deputy Sheriff, Warden, Jailer, Jail Physician and Detective Carroll accompanies Buck to the gallows. Those not permitted to attend the execution include an Indian who had earlier petitioned the Sheriff for admission, explaining that he wanted to tell his people about it. After being brought out of the cell, Buck shakes hands with the Sheriff and others in the corridor. A black silk cap is placed over his head. Father Cormier recites the usual prayer for the dying, and asks in the name of Buck forgiveness of all those he might have injured and the forgiveness of all in the world. Buck remains composed; he repeats after Father Cormier, "God have mercy on my soul and forgive me my sins." The priest adds, "I will meet you in heaven, Buck, where we will meet all our friends." The hangman steps forward and bids Buck good-bye. He then pulls the black cap over the doomed man's head. A voice is heard, "Go to heaven, Buck." "Thanks," Buck shouts. "Let her go; God have mercy on my soul." The hangman asks the priest if all is ready. "All ready; let him go to his God." Buck says, "Good-bye, gentlemen." Not masked himself, Radcliffe pulls the cord attached to the trip hook and Buck's body shoots into the air about four or five feet and falls again to the length of the rope with a slight thud. His feet are two feet from the ground. The legs and arms contract once or twice. A slight tremor occurs through the body.

After fourteen minutes Buck is pronounced dead. Father Cormier breaks down and sobs like a child. The hangman assures all that death has been instantaneous. It is a sad thing, he adds, but it is the fulfillment of the law and should be a warning to others. A half hour after the execution Buck's body is cut down and a coroner's inquest is held. There is some dispute over whether or not the neck has been broken. A post mortem is held. The bullet embedded in Buck's leg is removed. It proves to be a No. 38, the size of Jim's revolver. Buck's arms are found to be marked. On the left arm in blue are etched six American flags; on the right is tattooed an American eagle; over the eagle is a scroll or shield about an inch long. Buck's body is removed to the Catholic cemetery.

Speculations continued as to the real identity of Buck. Both Father Cormier and his defence counsel admitted that Olsen was not his real name. That Montreal's Detective Gross possessed a photo of Buck in his office, suggested that he was indeed one Buck Whelan who, with Jim Christie, was a well-known safe cracker in Quebec and the New England States.

As Radcliffe left for his home in Ontario a large crowd

gathered at the station to get one last look at the hangman. He was off to administer a fatal end to yet another murderer of a police officer — this time at Cornwall. That crowd soon lost interest, no doubt, in Buck's accomplice. Eventually transferred to the Kingston penitentiary, Jim died in the prison hospital's ward for the insane.

MURDER AT BEAR RIVER

On the morning of Tuesday, January 28th, 1896, another victim fell before the unrestrained passion of a killer — this time in the small village of Bear River. The mutilated body of a fifteen-year-old girl, Annie Kempton, was discovered in her house. Her father had been gone several days, lumbering near Lent Lake; her mother was away working in Worcester, Massachusetts. The condition of the victim's body was as horrible as that of Charlottetown's Callaghan eleven years earlier. The girl's skull was likewise severely bruised, with her throat cut from ear to ear.

The body was first discovered by a neighbour, Peter Wheeler. Detective Power, of Halifax, was summoned to help with the investigation. The girl's parents were both sent for. An inquest was quickly arranged. Although two men were held at Annapolis as possible suspects, the inquest concluded that enough circumstantial evidence pointed to Wheeler himself as the culprit. He was immediately arrested and taken to Digby where he was lodged in the jail.

At the inquest Wheeler had tried to suggest that strangers were responsible for the dastardly deed. Wheeler had been living in Bear River for twelve years, and boarded with Tillie Comeau on the Indian Hill road, only a few rods from the Kempton house. He said that on the previous Monday night he had slept by the fireplace. Awakening when the fire had gotten low, he claimed he had also heard voices outside. Looking out, he saw three men. Not thinking much of it, he went back to sleep. The next morning when he went for milk at Kempton's, as he rarely did, he found a stick of wood against the door. No one appeared when he opened the door. Moving from the kitchen to the next room, he found Annie lying on the floor. He said he thought she had fainted and

Annie Kempton
(Jo-Anne Stevens)

Peter Wheeler
(Jo-Anne Stevens)

Police officer Bowles
(Jo-Anne Stevens)

threw a coat over her. Inexplicably, he left her, but returned later. It was then that he noticed the blood and the gashes on the body. He immediately ran over to the house of Mrs. Omer Rice — this at about 8 a.m. on Tuesday morning — to sound the alarm. Bursting into her room, Wheeler said, "Mrs. Rice, do you know that Annie Kempton is lying dead on the floor with her throat cut?" The woman with her husband went to the Kempton house where they found the body. At the inquest Wheeler said he knew the victim well and that Tilly Comeau used to stay the night with Annie when her father was away. Wheeler indicated that Annie had told him Monday that Grace Morine would stay with her that night and not Tilly.

Wheeler's story was quickly suspect. The Morine girl denied that Annie had ever mentioned staying the night with her. Herbert Comeau, one of Tilly's sons, saw and spoke with Wheeler about dark that Monday night not far from the Kempton house. An Indian, Louis Jeremy, swore that he traced tracks from the Kempton house and found that they were made by "larigans," which Wheeler wore. Jeremy also testified that on Tuesday morning he went into Tilly Comeau's house directly after going to Kempton's. He encountered Wheeler.

> Wheeler was there when he went in and said he did not know who did the deed. He, Wheeler, said it must have been a tramp who wished to cover up the first wrong done the girl [i.e., rape] by murder; had he been the man, he said, he would rather serve 20 years in prison than be cast from Heaven. He, Wheeler, had shown Jeremy how the body lay when he found it. (The witness showed the court the position as stated by Wheeler, a half-kneeling position, arms on floor, left side of face on arms.) Wheeler told him that it didn't look well for people to see the body in that position and he had turned it over and put [a] coat around her. He had done it when he first went there.
>
> (The Digby Weekly Courier, 31 January 1896)

That this conflicted with Wheeler's own testimony added to the

Bear River, Nova Scotia, circa 1890. (PANS)

suspicion that he was the guilty party. The motive for the brutal crime was addressed by Stanley Rice, who had employed Wheeler for a short time at his lumber camp. Rice indicated he had heard Wheeler repeatedly state that "he would commit adultery with Annie the first time he got a chance, and was going to." Rice also denied that Wheeler, as he claimed, had been at his house at about the time it was supposed Annie had been murdered.

Wheeler did not help his own case as he was being conveyed to Digby by Detective Power:

> Wheeler dropped remarks to the effect that "something did not come out that may be some good to me. A respectable young fellow and I went up to Kempton's house that night. The young fellow wanted to go in, but I objected and we went back." He refused, however, the name of the young fellow. The detective returned to Harding Benson [who had testified at the inquest but had said nothing significant] as the young man referred to [and] secured from him a statement of some important facts that had not been included in his previous evidence.
>
> Interviewed, Benson admitted having gone to Kempton's house with Peter, starting from Tilly Comeau's.

Peter went in and wanted Benson to go in also but he refused and stopped at the gate and waited about a quarter of an hour, when Peter came out running and put his arms around Benson, and they then walked down the road together toward Tilly's house. Peter then cautioned Benson for his life not to tell anybody that they were at the house, and told him that Annie was then alone and advised him that he should go back and stay with her. Benson said he thought he would not go back and went home. Next day, after the body was found, Wheeler cautioned Benson not to say a word about this, as there were two knives on the floor and it would appear as if they had each used a knife. While the investigation was going on he sent word to him by a boy . . . not to mention anything about their being at Kempton's house that night.

(*The Digby Weekly Courier,* 7 February 1896)

The evidence suggested that Wheeler appeared to have gone to the Kempton house between five and six Monday evening after Annie's return from town. Finding her alone, he attacked her. Furious at her resistance, he hit her with a stick of wood. Later, concerned that she had perhaps survived, he enticed Benson to accompany him to the house with a view to implicating his friend in the deed. Unsuccessful, Wheeler went again into the house and cut Annie's throat, using two blunt dinner knives, hoping to make it seem that two persons had committed the crime.

The preliminary examination before the local magistrate at Digby called on a total of twenty-five witnesses. The prisoner was committed for trial for murder. The residents of Bear River expressed little doubt that he was guilty. Indeed their passionate demand for retribution forced a change of venue for the trial from Digby to Kentville. Judge Townshend, who made this decision, explained: "My duty is to see if possible that the trial in which the prisoner's life is at stake, takes place before a jury untainted with prejudice or foregone conclusions. After what I have heard and read it is impossible for me to think such a jury can be obtained when the feelings of the community, whence the jurors must be taken, have been so excited and worked upon by the press, always to the disadvantage of the accused" (*The Digby Weekly Courier,* 29 May 1896). The trial was scheduled for late June. Wheeler waited with apparent indifference, commenting that he was ready for it. The jailer, nonetheless, was requested to keep a close watch on him until the time of trial.

Wheeler, as he awaited his fate, may have reflected on his peripatetic life, and where it had brought him. He had been born in 1869 at Port Louis, the capital of the British island of Mauritius, off the southern coast of Africa. His father, Louis Wheeler, was an officer in the army. After his retirement he bought a small schooner, sailed as a packet around the island. The elder Wheeler's end was as tragic as that of his son; he succumbed to injuries caused by "a number of brutal companions." In addition, Wheeler's mother died quite suddenly.

While still a boy of only eight, Peter left home with an uncle for London. From there he went to St. Malo, France, where he took passage on a brig for a Scottish port. The young Wheeler spent eight months at the Glasgow Hospital, recovering from an injured foot. At the age of fifteen he left on a ship laden with coal for Barbados, where he found a home with a working family. He soon left again for passage to Digby. One of the sailors took him home to Bear River. But again his stay there was quite short. He found more permanent quarters at the house of Tilly Comeau, and was hired on by Isaac Kempton. From then to the time of the murder, he alternated with farmwork in the summer and winter and seafaring in the spring and fall. During this period his behaviour was described by acquaintances "as being of no noteworthy character, but as generally thought, a quiet, plodding, rough and unprogressive laborer's life." Many local residents at first found it difficult to believe that he had committed such a brutal act (*The Digby Weekly Courier,* 8 September 1896).

The trial at Kentville lasted only several days. Much of the evidence repeated what had been presented earlier at the inquest. Witnesses placed Wheeler at the Kempton home the night of the murder, Hardy Benson testified again of the accused's attempt to implicate him in the deed and others spoke of Wheeler's undisguised desires for the victim. After the counsels for defence and prosecution had rested their cases, Wheeler suddenly rose up in his seat and called out to the bench: "Your lordship, will you allow me to speak a word?" The judge responded: "Yes, through your counsel." The latter advised Wheeler to say nothing further.

The jury deliberated nearly two hours and returned with a guilty verdict. The courtroom became unusually hushed, the prisoner's face was pallid. The clerk asked the condemned man, "Have you anything to say why sentence of death should not be passed against you?" Wheeler stood up and answered, "I don't understand you. It is not because I am ignorant, but because I don't understand." After his counsel explained, Wheeler became silent. The judge pronounced the sentence:

> I hope you will now pay great attention to what I have to say to you. The jury have convicted you of the murder of Annie Kempton and in their finding I concur. You have had a fair trial and every effort has been made on your behalf to establish your innocence and a patient jury has given it the fullest investigation. The jury was not from the place where the crime was committed, and consequently were not prejudiced, and have clearly brought this awful crime against you. Probably the most hard thing to do is for one man to pass sentence of death upon another. I cannot help thinking of the cruel way the poor girl was murdered. I will give you ample time to repent for the crime of which you have been found guilty. I only hope and pray that you may devote the remaining few weeks in preparation for the future world. I do not know your religious views, but I do sincerely hope you will be repentant. I hereby direct that you be taken hence to the jail in Kentville and thence to the jail in Digby and detained there till the 8th day of September, 1896, and on that day hanged by the neck till dead.

(*The Digby Weekly Courier*, 3 July 1896)

The prisoner, in a clear voice, responded: "I hope you will find

out who the guilty party is before that time." Despite such protes-
tation of innocence, only a few days later Wheeler made a full
confession to the murder. The details of his story, however, varied
according to whom he subsequently spoke. The "real facts" he acknowledged in the end were to be contained in a statement to be
made public only after his execution. This statement was obtained
through the assistance of Digby's Police Officer Bowles, who in
the end apparently acted as Wheeler's "spiritual advisor." Bowles
was a prominent member of the local branch of the Salvation Army
and was able to develop some rapport with the condemned man,
suggesting the multifaceted role of a police officer in a late
nineteenth-century small town. Bowles was asked whether Wheeler
was really as repentant as he seemed:

> I do and I believe that his confession as you are printing
> it is true. I know that people seem to think it impossible
> for such a fellow to sincerely repent but from what I have
> seen of him I believe he has. I have spent a good deal of
> time with him and have studied him carefully. I have
> taken him on every tack and have been severe as well as
> kind with him. Some people have gone to him, spent five
> or ten minutes and formed their opinion of him accord-
> ingly; in most cases they have formed it before coming.
> I have watched him closely, have tried to show him his
> true position and to give him what guidance I could. He
> always received my efforts attentively and while I do not
> know if he has ever fully realized the awfulness of his
> position I sincerely believe he is repentant and has
> received a measure of comfort. His crime was a terrible
> one, and he has come to see it so himself. His confession
> is a reasonable one and I believe it is true. My opinion
> comes of a close observation of the man without
> prejudice.

(*The Digby Weekly Courier,* 8 September 1896)

Wheeler's confession contained some new "facts" not heretofore known and not totally consistent with the testimony of other
witnesses. He sought to explain his own motive for the deed:

PETER WHEELER'S CONFESSION

On the 27th of January I left home about 11 o'clock in the forenoon. I went up to hunt for some wood. When I got in front of
Kempton's gate Annie came to the front door and called to me and
asked me where Tilly [Comeau] was and I told her that Tilly and
Hattie [Tilly's daughter] were both to the hotel to work. She then
wanted to know if they were going to be away all week and I said
I did not know, only that they had said so. Then Annie said, "You
tell Tilly that as she is to be away all the week she needn't mind
coming away up here nights. After working from home all day and
coming home and looking after the children, and then away up this
hill, she will be too tired. I will try to get (I understood her to say)
Grace Morine because it will just be fun for her to come here and
stay nights.

Then she asked me if I knew whether the sleighing party was
coming up from Digby to Bear River the forenoon or afternoon of
the next day. I said I did not know which but that it was some time
in the day. Then she asked me in. I went and shortly afterward she
got her dinner. She had baked beans and asked me if I would have
some with her but I thanked her and refused taking any. After talking a while I went home, at about noon. I made a fire, got my
dinner and baked four loaves of bread. Shortly after Annie passed
back home, as she had gone down to the village for some tissue
paper.

At fifteen minutes after five I started and went up and around
by Mrs. Omer Rice's and around the Harris Hollow, as it was said
in the evidence, and around to where Elmer Crabbe saw me, which
is more like an hour's walk than twenty minutes; and across the
Parker road down to the field, back of barn, and under barn. While
I was there Annie came in and fed and milked the cow and when
she went in the house with the milk I started running down the
road.

I met Herbert Comeau and stayed and helped the little fellow
where he was cutting wood. I loaded his sled and then we started
for home. When we got there Matilda and Hattie had just got back
from the hotel. I told Tilly what Annie had said about getting the

Morine girl to stay with her and Tilly said she was glad of it for she was tired. Then Tilly, Walter, Hattie and myself started for the Bridge. On our way Crabbe overtook us and we went along almost to the Bridge. Then Hattie and her mother and Walter went their way and I went mine. I went to Mr. W.R. Rice's shop to purchase what little things I needed to go in the woods next day.

When I left Mr. Rice's shop it was 25 minutes to 8 o'clock. I met Walter and while I was talking to him Benson came along and asked me how long before I was going home. I said pretty soon. Then I started to go for Tilly but turned back and Benson and I started for the flat. Benson asked me if I had seen Annie that night and I said that I had seen her in the afternoon. Then he said that he had been looking for her around the Salvation Army and wanted to know whether she was home or not. I said I did not know. Then I told him that Annie said she was going to try and get Grace Morine to stay with her for it was too much for Tilly to work all day from home and then trace up the hill. When we got in front of Tilly's house Benson proposed for us to go to Kempton's to see if Annie was home and if she was coming out. So we started and went up. When we got to the electric light dam we saw the light at Kempton's and there was nothing said about, "I'll stop here and you go on," but both went along together as far as the gate. I never went ahead of Benson. When we got to the gate Benson said, "Peter, you go in. I'll wait here but don't let on to Annie that I am here and don't stay long." I said no and started running; went in porch (also called the kitchen) and I stood there and asked her if she was coming out to meeting that night. She asked why. I said someone was there waiting. She asked who and if it was Benson. I said, "Yes but don't let on I told you," and she said, "No." She went to the front door and looked out the sidelights and saw him and came back and said that she would get ready right away and afterwards said, "Tell Herbert to come up and stay with me." Just before I left she said again, "Herbert need not come. I guess I can do." I said good night and started back running to where Benson was and put my arms around him. Then he asked me if I had asked Annie what he was doing. I said no, and he wanted to know if the

Morine girl was there. I said no, that she was alone and that she said she was coming right out. "Go in and wait for her," I said. He answered, "No, don't let on to anyone we went up here." I asked why and he said, "I don't like for anyone to know that I came around here nights when Annie's alone." I said, "I'll never tell you were there. Go in and wait for her," but he said no. I said that if I was going with a girl and looking for her to come out I would wait for her. He said, "Some other time." Friends, I wish Benson had have come in and waited. She would have come out. Then I would not have known whether she had come out with him or not and I would not have gone back in the night. Anyway we left the Kemptons' gate, on our way down home. When we got to the electric light corner Benson said to wait till we saw if her light was out but it was then burning bright. We went down to Tilly Comeau's house. Herbert Comeau and Herbert Rice were there alone for Tilly or Hattie or Walter had not returned from the bridge the second time. Benson and I came out and stood at the gate. Hattie and Walter came along shortly afterward and Benson started for home. Then Tilly came along and she and Benson stood a few minutes talking. They were about 30 or 40 rods from the Comeau gate where I stood. I said to Tilly, "I've heard tell of brown cows coming home one after the other"; can't say what she answered. Hattie and Walter went in the house and Tilly, Benson and I came behind with the sled. Tilly said to Benson, "Have you seen Annie today, or do you know whether she is home or not?" He said he had seen her about 4 o'clock at the bridge but he did not know whether she was home or not.

It was about a quarter after eight when Benson went home. I went out to the gate with him and said good night, then went into the house and washed some meat, and put on to cook, to take to the woods next day. I made my bed on the floor next to the stove as I had been used to doing through the winter for my room was so far from the stove. Can't say who went to bed first, Tilly or I. Think I was lying on the quilts when she went to bed. About half an hour after Mr. Benson went home from the electric light station, I heard people talking down towards the corner. I got up and went into the sitting room and looked down the road and saw quite a lot of people at the corner and at the foot of Indian Hill. Then I went back to the kitchen and got a big block of wood and put against the door, and some mats, so that the wind would not blow the door back and forth; and I went to the stair door and put a chair and a stand against it for the wind was blowing quite hard that night. Then I went to the curtains and rolled them up and raised the window up a little at a time. I was quite a little while doing that on account of not making too much noise for Tilly was not a sound sleeper. After I got the window raised I put a stick under it and went back into kitchen and dressed myself and started and went running. Lord forgive me for it. I saw no one and no one saw me but the Almighty. That's why I said that all the stories E.P. Parker, Omer Rice, Louis Jeremy, Stanley Rice, Myrtle Godfrey and Hardy Benson told about me will never condemn me. God is the only witness that saw me, or knows anything about it. I went to the door and knocked and heard no answer. I stood in the path beneath the window and called to Annie and she answered and asked, "Who is it?" I said, "Peter." Then she said, "Why didn't you stay home? I was just to sleep good." I told her then that the rest of them would be up by and by for there were a crowd of drunkards around and we were afraid so I had started and come up. I asked her to open the door and she said, "I'll be right there in a minute." She opened and I went in. She went and showed me how many bunches of flowers she had made and she said she had not been to bed long. She started and went back to bed. We were then in the dark. I stood in the sitting room and we had quite a talk with each other. Can't say what we were saying but I remember telling her that I had heard and seen people down to the corner and to the foot of Indian Hill until after half past twelve o'clock that night. There had been no harm said between Annie and me during that time until that monster Satan got to go in her room. There's where the first of the fracas took place. I tried to keep her in the room but she was too quick and strong for me. I tried to hold her from going into the sitting room and she caught hold of the table and upset it and everything on it. Among the things that were on the table was a milk pan which was filled with the night's milk. That was broken on the floor and Annie and I both fell with her face on the broken milk pan and she cut her hand and the side of her head and also her forehead. Then she tried to light the lamp and I pulled her away from it and she dropped the chimney. She tried also to get matches off the mantel piece and she wanted to get matches in the pantry to find some saleratus to put on her cut face and hand. That's how come the blood on the chimney and matches. Then she went into the bedroom to try to raise the window but I would not let her. She went to window towards Bern Rice's, that is the window facing the electric dam, and I would not let her. She then started to go into the porch, when the key was broken. She tried several times to light the lamp and to raise the windows and could not. I will also explain to you how that blood got on the piece of tissue paper. The first or second time that Annie went to the window towards the electric dam she took the piece of tissue paper off the stand and wiped her face with it and threw it down for she was then bleeding quite badly out the side of her head and her hand which she cut upon the broken milk pan. It was one of those earthen pans and the milk was spilt on the floor. I did not accomplish lust nor she had not been struck by me then. She then wanted to light the lamp for the last time. Then she said, "Peter, I will never tell on you, if you will let me alone," and I felt then like stopping. Something says, "Don't you." Then we got into another tussle and she said, "Peter, kill me." It was a very hard blow when I heard that word. I said, "Why Annie do you want to die?" "Yes, kill me." And it was still harder for me when I took that stick and hit her, and the knife to finish the deed the way I did. I only struck her with the stick once, I think, and that was on the side near the back of the head. She then laid on the floor just where she was found and I was on the opposite side of her when her throat was cut. It was almost like driving a knife into my own heart. But it wasn't me alone or I would have never got up out of bed and done what I did. It was that dreadful Satan. He is the cause of a good many men's and women's ruin, if not in one way, in another.

I washed my hands in the Kempton porch before leaving. This

was just half past one o'clock on the morning of January 28. I
started then running for home. There was no light when I got to
Kempton's nor while I was there nor after I left. I expect I was five
minutes going from their home. I crawled back into the window the
same way I crawled out and went into the kitchen where my bed
was and lit the lamp. It wanted twenty minutes to two o'clock. I
asked Tilly if she heard someone talking; she said yes. I shortly afterwards went into the room and put the window down and
unrolled the curtains and placed things on the table as I had found
them before going up to Kempton's, and also the doors, and went
back to bed. No one saw me going or coming and I saw no one.
The Lord is the only witness and detective who knows anything
about it and he is a true witness. I am also writing a true confession
before him. I never realized what I had done until after I came
from Kempton's after the milk. Tilly said, "Will you go after the
milk?" I said yes and started and when I went in and saw the state
the room was in it appeared strange to me. I still did not believe
that she was dead until I put my hand on the side of her forehead;
then it came back to me, "See, Peter, what you have done." I tell
you friends you might think that I am just talking but if it had been
my own mother or sister I would not have felt any worse than I did
when I saw poor Annie lying on the floor and knew that I could
not speak to her nor she to me. I could have stood there and had
twice the same thing done to me.

I understood that the people won't believe that this accident
took place in the middle of the night. What good would it be to me
to sit down and write a lot of lies? It would be a queer way to seek
repentance. What does it say in Romans, xiv, 10? I suppose you all
remember that Tilly Comeau said she thinks that I was lying on the
quilts with my clothes on when she went to bed. That will give you
more of an idea and would make you understand that it was done
in the middle of the night. Remember I also said in my evidence
that I lighted the lamp in the night and it wanted twenty minutes
to two o'clock. I was just home then from Kempton's. I also made
a fire; it was then that I examined my clothes and washed off what
little blood was on them. The next morning I came and alarmed

Tilly and from there I kept on going around telling the people. On my way back the thoughts struck me about the tracks I had made in the night in coming and going to Kempton's, from out of the little room window. I said then to myself they will follow my tracks clean to the window and I will be found out. I must go home and look after it. When I got home Tilly and the children had gone up to Kempton's. I started around the house and stepped in the same tracks and there was no blood in them. I went to the window and made believe to raise it so if they wanted to know how came the tracks there I would then say that I had come to go into the house and found Tilly and the children had gone out and I had gone around to try to get in the window.

Friends and strangers I will now again ask you to take warning. If I have done evil all my life and end it in doing evil there is no need of anyone else doing the same. The best and the only cure for anyone in darkness through sins and evil is for them to get right with God and his boundless love and mercy will keep you from trouble.

Young men, I pray you take warning of this same first temptation. If you are ever so tempted remember poor Peter Wheeler and that lust caused him to do brutality and murder. Remember, friends, don't let Satan run away with you as he did with me for he is very cute and ready to tempt us and to get us in trouble; but he is very cowardly at the end and is sure to leave us in the lurch.

I don't wish to tell anything false about the poor girl for I have done enough. I wish that I had not accomplished any of the temptation but Satan, the dreadful brute, leads us from one thing to another as he did me that night. A girl who was a friend to me! I can't forgive myself for what I have done. I was always treated well by her father and mother and also her sisters. Friends I can't explain why it had to be poor Annie. There are lots of girls and men and women in Bear River who hated me; why couldn't it have been someone else beside her? I can't understand. I could not see at the time for Satan had me blinded until it was too late. Beware of him, friends; don't be blinded by him. Always try to remember poor Peter Wheeler and try to keep in the light and don't be in darkness, that is, in sins and he won't have you blinded. For the longer you are in sins the blinder you are. I was warned lots of times in my own feelings to get right with God and was also warned by others but I rejected the warning and stayed in darkness. Oh my dear friends don't refuse to give up your sinful ways of living which leads us all to captivity and ruin. Be wise; when God knocks at your heart's door and offers you his light, which is salvation, freely, accept of it. If anyone had to buy it we might have an excuse and say we are too poor but it is free to all, without money or price.

Peter D. Wheeler

(*The Digby Weekly Courier,* 8 September 1896)

Wheeler elaborated on the above in an interview he gave shortly before he was executed. He denied that the crime was premeditated. He was asked why he went under the Kempton barn at five o'clock in the afternoon of the day of the murder. He was told it was thought he was there to spy.

"A queer place for spying," he answered. "I was there for eggs."

"Had you ever been there for eggs before?"

"No."

"Then how was it you happened there that day?"

"Because while I had been talking with Annie at noon she had said the hens were laying there. I was wanting to get some eggs for the woods the next day and just then the devil put it into my head that there was the place to get my eggs. Then late in the afternoon I heard the hens cackling and I started on the steal and went up around and under the barn."

"Then you say Annie came in to milk the cow. Could you see her?"

"No, but I heard her and I was where she would have seen the light if I had struck a match."

"Well then if you did not have it all planned through the day when did you? Didn't you think about Annie's being alone and that Tilly wasn't going up? And why did you go to bed dressed if you didn't plan to get up in the night?"

"I didn't undress because Tilly was around. It never came into my head to go up there until I woke up at twelve. Then the devil seemed to say it was a good time for me to carry out the threats I had made."

"You didn't plan to kill her then?"

"No, I certainly did not. I never thought of it."

"Wasn't it risky in your leaving the window up while you were gone? Suppose Tilly had waked up and found you had left?"

"It was risky but I never stopped to think about that and the devil seemed to help me."

"Annie believed your story about the crowd of drunks did she?"

"Yes, of course. She had put a wrapper on before she came to the door. I had worked with her father and knew the family well, and she had full confidence in me that, as a neighbour and an old employee of her father, I wanted nothing that would be wrong. I lied to her about the crowd as an excuse for disturbing her, and so I could get in."

"How many blows did you strike her?"

"That is the one thing I don't remember exactly. I can't say. The devil had such a hold on me I was beside myself."

"Do you expect that the people will believe that Annie asked you to kill her just as if it were a pleasure?"

"I don't know what the people will believe. I only know I am telling the truth and God knows it is true. Annie said, 'Peter, kill me.' "

"Didn't she say it as if she meant she would rather be killed than submit to your abuse? Wasn't she frantic with pain?"

"She was crying terribly. Of course she was suffering, for the pain from the blows must have been awful."

"Suppose that Tilly had not sent you for milk the next morning would you have gone up to the house or left it for someone else to find?"

"I would have left it for someone else I think."

"Peter are you really sorry for your crime or only because you have to die for it?"

"I am sorry from my heart. If I had been myself I would never have done the deed and I didn't realize what I had done for a long time. I know my sentence is right. I deserve to die and hanging is too good for me."

"Would you rather be kept in prison for life?"

"No. I feel that I ought to die more as I have caused Annie Kempton to die."

"Are you afraid of your coming punishment?"

"No. I do not feel a fear of death. It's right that it should come."

(*The Digby Weekly Courier,* 8 September 1896)

This confession did not mollify the public. Wheeler's execution was scheduled by Digby's Sheriff B. VanBlarcom for the morning of September 8th, between the hours of seven and eight o'clock. The night before, the Sheriff was awakened by an informer who told him that a mob of two or three hundred was gathering. It was their intention at dawn the next day to seize the prisoner and lynch him in a public area. VanBlarcom quickly decided to put the execution forward to an earlier hour. The doctor, coroner and jurors were notified. Wheeler finished his last meal and dressed himself in new clothing — a pair of black pants, white shirt and a pair of patent leather shoes. A black cap was placed over his head, drawn tightly down to the shoulders; a three-quarter inch rope encircled his neck. The gallows had been designed especially for the occasion by the Sheriff:

> The rope, one end of which was the noose, passed up from the death chamber through the ceiling, which is the floor of the front porch, over a pulley, across a few feet

over another pulley, through the floor again where about two feet below hung four big pieces of lump-lead, weighing 500 pounds. The end of the rope was brought up again through the floor and fastened, thus holding the weight.

(*The Digby Weekly Courier*, 8 September 1896)

When the Sheriff cut the rope, the drop-weights fell to the ground, the rope tightened over the pulleys and Wheeler's body shot upward more than two feet. At 2:45 a.m. his body was cut down and the murderer was pronounced dead.

At daybreak, carriages brought many from the surrounding countryside. Their view of the spectacle, however, was to be denied. All they could do was await completion of the monument to be erected in Mount Hope Cemetery, in memory of the young victim. A committee was organized, with subscriptions solicited in many of the neighboring towns. With the money raised a stone was ordered from Saint John. The inscription to be placed on it was to read:

ERECTED TO THE MEMORY OF ANNIE KEMPTON
Who was murdered in her father's house,
in a desperate struggle to preserve her chastity.
January 27, 1896.

The subscribers hereby express their profound respect for the heroine who maintained unto death the sacred honour of womanhood, one of the highest virtues of a Christian civilization.

(*The Digby Weekly Courier*, 8 September 1896)

The tragedy at Bear River had ended. But this was little comfort for the victim's family. Mrs. Kempton's spirit was said to have been broken; soon after, she became seriously ill. The residents of Digby and Bear River returned to the routine of their lives, still shocked that such brutality could occur in their ostensibly peaceful domain.

THE MEADOW BROOK TRAGEDY

Only days after Peter Wheeler's execution the Maritimes were visited with another "crime of horror." The peacefulness of the small village of Meadow Brook, twelve miles outside Moncton, was shattered by a double murder that also involved arson and robbery.

Mrs. James Green did not sleep well the night of Thursday, September 10th, 1896. She laid awake on the bed listening to the periodic barking of her dog from ten o'clock on. Her insomnia, she later related, also reflected a general nervousness and fear of the tramps who had been seen in the area. Meadow Brook was on the I.C.R. line that connected Moncton, Calhoun Station and Memramcook; and a railroad line brought itinerant strangers. At approximately 2 a.m. the restless woman heard a wagon crossing the bridge nearby. Curious at who was passing through, she left her bed to peer through the blinds. Across the way in another house, little more than 125 yards distant, she spotted a light in the bedroom of her sister-in-law, Mrs. Eliza Dutcher. At first she thought nothing of this. As the light grew brighter, she realized the awful truth. She immediately aroused her own three children, ran out of the house down the road, raising the cry of fire. Hugh Green, a neighbor and brother of Mrs. Dutcher, heard the alarm and ran toward the burning house. "For God's sake, get an axe," he yelled at Mrs. Green. He found the front door locked. With the aid of the axe, he broke it in, and ran through the kitchen. At the stairway he was momentarily stopped by the spreading smoke, but saw no fire until he reached the bedroom upstairs, where Mrs. Dutcher, her eleven-year-old son Harris, and nine-year-old daughter Maggie slept together. At first Green could see no one through the flames and smoke. Groping his way along, he soon heard the cry, "Mamma, Mamma" from the little girl. Following the direction of her voice, he soon was able to locate the child. Her hair and eyebrows were singed by fire. He carried her quickly downstairs, and handed her over to his own daughters. Green ran back to see if he could save Mrs. Dutcher and her son, but the fire was now too intense to return to the second floor. He had been too excited to return to the burning building to notice that the girl he had saved was not only suffering from burns; Annie's skull had been crushed and her left ear had been split as if cut with a knife. The child was carried unconscious to her uncle's house. A doctor was summoned immediately. As he dressed her wounds, she cried out in agony, "Oh, don't kill me any more." Her chances of survival did not appear strong.

The fire continued unchecked. Neighbours gathered, watching helplessly as the building crumbled. The floor of the upstairs bedroom finally caved in, bringing with it the bodies of the slain mother and son. Their cremation was thorough. Sifting through the ashes later, after the fire had abated, the men discovered the trunk of a body about two feet in length. Mrs. Dutcher's head and limbs had been completely consumed. Some charred bones, the portion of a skull, and a few bone ashes — all that remained of her son — were placed in a small basket for later examination. Not located was any trace of the trustworthy Dutcher watchdog, "Kiss," whose disappearance remained mysterious to all.

The injuries Annie had suffered immediately suggested that this had not been an accidental fire. The motive of the crime was assumed to be robbery. Mrs. Dutcher, suspicious of the possible insolvency of banking institutions, kept all her money — estimated by family and visitors to be between $400 and $500 — in a small trunk in her room. The robber, it was speculated, murdered the woman, and then tried to cover up the crime by resorting to arson.

The Dutcher house was not a stranger to the law. The family had moved there some years earlier. Mrs. Dutcher's husband, a millwright, had himself built their house, but had died in 1893. His wife was a Green, whose neighbours included two brothers, James and Hugh. Mrs. Dutcher's was a "roadhouse," where liquor was illegally sold. The police had prosecuted her several times for Scott Act violations. On one occasion she had served 45 days in jail, refusing to pay a fine that had been imposed. She and her brother Hugh had not been on speaking terms for some time, apparently over some dispute about a case of whiskey. Although he had himself sold liquor at one time, Hugh believed his sister had kept a rough house and did not want his children visiting there.

All through the day after the fire, numerous residents of Moncton and surrounding districts flocked to the ruins of the house. Walking around the edge of the cellar and poking through the ashes in search of other traces of the cremated bodies, they were struck with the horror of the crime. William Dutcher, who had arrived from Nova Scotia after being advised of his mother's death, also sifted through the ashes. He quickly found some $45 in gold pieces. Insofar as they had not been greatly blackened by the fire and smoke, speculation arose that perhaps the murderer had returned after the fire to place them there and thus suggest that no robbery had occurred but only an accidental fire. As this inspection of the ruins continued, the remains of Mrs. Dutcher and her son were buried in the nearby Catholic cemetery.

Within a day of the tragedy, suspicion focused on John Sullivan, son of Daniel Sullivan, a resident of Moncton, as the alleged murderer. Some enmity had apparently existed between the Greens and the Sullivans. Mrs. Jane Green reported that Mrs. Dutcher had told her she had been visited by John early Thursday morning, a day before the fire:

> He asked her if she had anything to drink, she replied that she had not a drop in the house. He then asked her if she had any cigars and she said yes. He told her to come down and give him some and he would pay her a little debt he owed her. She went into the bed-room and he asked her if she had any ale and she said she thought she had one bottle; he got the bottle and two cigars and paid her for them, but he did not pay the debt. He took one cigar and left the other on the counter. He said he was

going to Geo. McPhee's to stay all night. She next saw him coming down the track Thursday morning. She said she didn't care much about him; that was the reason she did not like to let him in. She was that afraid of him that she took her pocket book out of her pocket and put it under her children's feet before she came downstairs. She was afraid he might knock her down and take it away from her.

(*The Moncton Daily Times,* 16 September 1896)

Whether or not Mrs. Green was correctly echoing her slain sister-in-law's fears of him, the supposition that Sullivan had been the assailant gained support as he could not be immediately located. His father tried to quell the rumours, indicating John had been at his house in Moncton the night of the fire, but had left town Saturday night. His destination was unclear.

As preparations were made for the inquest, Coroner Wortman received a telegram from Solicitor-General White to delay the proceedings until his arrival. The cause of the tragedy now attracted province-wide interest. The inquiry commenced at 11:30 a.m. September 15th in an unoccupied building near the scene of the fire. Aside from the Solicitor-General, F.A. McCully was present on behalf of the crown. Dozens of neighbours and a few Monctonians attended. For the next two weeks more than sixty witnesses were called, giving 128 pages of foolscap in testimony, the lengthiest inquest ever experienced by the Coroner.

Sullivan's activities in the hours following the fire were not such as to convince temperance advocates of his respectability:

Sullivan was in Moncton at 5 o'clock on the morning of the Meadow Brook tragedy, near O.S. Legere's place of business on Lower Main street. He encountered Charles Colborne who remarked to Sullivan that he was looking very "seedy," and asked him if he had been out all night, whereupon Sullivan replied that he had been down on the wharves with the girls. Between 6 and 7 o'clock Sullivan entered O.S. Legere's bar and took a "soldier" and was about to take another when he recognized Colborne in the sitting room and an old chap in the bar who was talking to Andrew Melanson. Sullivan promptly extended an invitation to Colborne and the old fellow to drink, but having never met Melanson before he asked the old man to bring up his partner. Melanson willingly joined them and before the party broke up Sullivan had treated six or seven times. His companions of the hour say that he appeared to be "flush," so much so that a young man named White, who knew Sullivan very well, asked him where he was working. Sullivan replied that he was not working anywhere now, which caused young White to say that he was lucky to have so much money for a man who was not working. Sullivan appeared to have $4 or $5 in silver and changed a $5 bill while in Legere's. Sullivan told Melanson and Colborne a story about losing $5 in changing a $10 bill Thursday night [this apparently to establish an alibi that he had been in Moncton and not Meadow Brook the night of the fire]. He thought it lost it at his uncle's, he said, indicating the Queen Hotel. Colborne and he afterward went to the Queen to enquire after the missing $5, but was convinced by the clerk that the $5 had not been lost there. Not only was the $5 not lost there, but Mr. McKinnon [the Hotel proprietor] stated that he is not Sullivan's uncle, and Sullivan was not at his house at all on Thursday night. None of the clerks seem to remember the man either.

During Friday forenoon [the morning of the fire] Sullivan [with Colborne and Melanson] went in Mr. Richard's barber shop. He pulled out a handful of silver to pay for the shave [of himself and his two companions], and remarked to Mr. Richard that he guessed he would pay for a month's shaving in advance. Mr. Richard thinks Sullivan must have had a couple pieces of American silver. Richard says he remembers that there appeared to be something troubling the man, and he was on the point of asking him once or twice but refrained. Sullivan, Melanson and Colborne after leaving the barber shop went up to Melanson's house on Telegraph Street, where they ate a raw fish apiece. From there Sullivan and Colborne went to the Queen and later started out to buy some clothing [Sullivan's clothes, Colborne later testified, appeared to be considerably dishevelled] at W.D. Martin's. He purchased a pair of pants and had them sent up to his father's house on High Street. He paid for the goods with two fifty cent pieces and quarters. Mr. Harvey, the clerk, says he had some difficulty in getting Sullivan to tell him his name to put on the parcel. Finally Colborne gave the information. Sullivan was then pretty full. Sullivan showed up at O.S. Legere's again Saturday morning and treated a couple of friends a couple of times.

(*The Moncton Daily Times,* 16 September 1896)

Sullivan's generosity in buying the rounds only made him more suspect. The Wednesday before the fire was his last day of work at Anderson's mill, where he received the balance in wages due him — $1.22. A week before that he had been paid $8. Apparently Sullivan was hopeful of getting back on the I.C.R. as a brakeman. Hearing of his lavish expenditures, William Dutcher, the slain woman's son, launched his own investigation. That Sullivan had displayed several pieces of American silver, of the same type he recalled which had been in his mother's possession, was not taken as merely circumstantial evidence.

Sullivan's parents continued to defend him. His mother testified that she had heard her son coming in Thursday in the middle of the night. He did not go to bed. She first saw him the next morning after he had purchased the new pants, carrying a bundle of the old clothes he had worn. Both parents denied knowing where he now was, although they later admitted they had encouraged him to leave town immediately and stay with his uncle in Maine.

The lengthy inquest left Maggie, still semi-conscious, untouched, but not ignored. Numbers of the curious visited her six-by-eight-foot room to view the victim's wounds. It was evident that she required better medical attention than she had been receiving. The Solicitor-General dispatched Dr. Ross to care for her and instructed him to assign an experienced nurse for the child. Anna Croasdale and her sister Muriel remained with Maggie, trying to help nurse her back to health. The urgent need for a hospital in Moncton at this time was made more evident to many. That Maggie's testimony was critical in identifying the assailant encouraged these ministrations. Lapsing in and out of consciousness, some of the child's utterances seemed especially damaging:

> When she awakens she evinces great terror and will cling to the person trying to sooth her imploring her to be protected from some monster. In her delirium she has given utterance to a few things which the crown consider to be of great importance. Recently she startled those in the room by crying out "Go away John Sullivan." At other times she shrieks "Don't kill me." At such times she is very much agitated and terrified.

(*The Moncton Daily Times,* 19 September 1896)

Three days after the inquest had commenced, a warrant was issued for Sullivan's arrest as a material witness. Although he had suggested to some that Nova Scotia was his destination, he was quickly located at his uncle's house in Alexander, Maine. At first resisting arrest, he was taken to the lock-up at Calais. Sullivan, claiming that he had come to Maine to attend to the division of some property, at first refused to return to Moncton of his own consent. This would have involved extradition proceedings that could have taken several weeks to complete, but proved unnecessary. R.B. Smith, who had been engaged to defend the accused, gave Sullivan's father a letter to take to the son advising him to return to Moncton "without putting the Canadian authorities to the trouble of extraditing him." Sullivan relented, but still indicated he hated to return, saying they "are such a prejudiced lot up there." Sheriff McQueen brought the prisoner back to Moncton by train. Their arrival at the station was greeted by a large crowd. Affecting a rather jovial manner, Sullivan shook hands with his brother and nodded to acquaintances. Several hundred people followed him as he walked without handcuffs to the police station.

Sullivan's appearance at the inquest caused considerable commotion. He showed little emotion as he listened to the continuing proceedings. Periodically, the Coroner asked him if he was willing to testify; each time he steadfastly refused.

After the last witness had been summoned, the jury retired, and returned in little more than an hour with the verdict "that Eliza Dutcher and Harris Dutcher came to their deaths by foul means and we have reasonable grounds to believe and do believe from the evidence submitted that John E. Sullivan was implicated in the same" (*The Moncton Daily Times,* 28 September 1896).

The case against Sullivan was sent to Moncton's police court for preliminary examination. W.H. Fry, the Supreme Court stenographer, was brought in to keep a record of the proceedings. That he was skilled in shorthand meant the hearing was held more quickly than usual. The setting was not an attractive one either for those in court or in the lock-up:

> Those who have had occasion to visit the lockup and police court room of late could not have failed to notice their filthy condition. The stench in the lockup is almost unbearable and in the police court room it is little better when crowded as it has been of late. The building is unfit for occupation of man or beast and the most ill-kept stable would be a rose garden in comparison with the lockup. It is shame to put the most debased criminal in the lockup in its present condition while the health of the magistrate and court attendants generally must be seriously imperilled by the atmosphere of the court room. The city fathers should be confined for at least a quarter of an hour within the precincts of the Duke street edifice. If they were it is quite certain that a supply of deodorizers would be at once ordered and some steps taken to keep the air reasonably pure by ventilation.
>
> (*The Moncton Daily Times,* 3 October 1896)

Moncton's City Council immediately instructed the Police

Committee to enlist the services of the engineer to develop a plan of renovation. Sullivan did not have to endure the stench long. On October 3rd he was transferred to the county jail at Dorchester.

Jane Green, Hugh Green, Charles Colborne and many others who had testified at the inquest repeated, with some elaboration, what they had said earlier. T.B. Calhoun told the court he had been in Mrs. Dutcher's house about the 12th of August, and had seen her with a large roll of bills — estimated at about $400 or $500. Calhoun confirmed her disreputable business; many of his millmen bought liquor from her and frequently got drunk at the Dutcher house on Sundays.

Court adjourned for one day as Sullivan fell ill, seized with a fit of vomiting. His alleged victim remained in poor condition. The attending doctors agreed it was not wise to operate. In an effort to secure more comfortable arrangements for her, Dr. Ross brought Maggie to Moncton, where she was placed in an isolated room at the almshouse. It was evident that her condition was such that she would not have been able to testify for at least several weeks more. That did not prevent someone from attempting to enter the almshouse several hours after midnight one Monday during her confinement. Whether this was an attempt to abduct her or the misbehavior of common drunks was unclear. Authorities took no chance and assigned Officer Trites to guard her. She continued to express a fear of being left alone, being heard to say, "He might come upstairs again." She did not identify who "he" was.

The circumstantial evidence against Sullivan continued to mount. A hotel keeper identified the accused as the man he met in Saint John several days after the fire and recalled that he had been in possession of a large roll of bills. An I.C.R. conductor denied Sullivan's claim that he had been on the train which arrived in Moncton the evening of September 10th. Ardina Howell testified that Daniel Sullivan had urged her to swear that she had met his son when the train had arrived that night. Later when she did have contact with John, he told her "the fire was a fact because he had come from there that morning." The interweaving of these statements left little doubt in the mind of Detective Carroll, who had years earlier apprehended the infamous "Jim." In town on other business, the Pictou policeman believed there was enough evidence to convict Sullivan of murder. In contrast, the parents continued to protest the innocence of their son. Mrs. Sullivan told the Court that she had been responsible for having Mrs. Dutcher sent to Dorchester for selling liquor on the Sabbath. "They [the Greens] had a spite on me and they would have revenge on the family." Jane Green in particular, she added, could not be trusted.

Although she had recovered somewhat, Maggie still did not appear well enough to testify. Several days before this preliminary examination ended, the Crown decided that she should not be brought in as a witness until the case was transferred to the Supreme Court in January. This did not sit well with the defence:

Stipendiary Wortman: Do you wish to call any witnesses, Mr. Smith?

Mr. Smith: Yes, your worship, there is a most important witness we want to call and that is Maggie Dutcher, and if it is possible I would like to have the case adjourned for eight days. In the meantime I would like to have Dr. Chandler or some other doctor besides the crown doctor to examine Maggie Dutcher to see if she is fit to give evidence. We would like to have the evidence of Maggie Dutcher. It is exactly what John Sullivan wants and what I want. For this reason I would like to have the case adjourned for eight days, and if the girl is able to give evidence then we will call her. If she is not fit, then we won't call her.

Stipendiary Wortman: How would it do to call some other witness? You have the accused right on the spot, why not put him on.

Mr. Smith: I do not propose to call any other witnesses just now. I have a right to call Maggie Dutcher and propose to do it. We want some doctor to examine the child in the interests of the prisoner to see if she is able to give evidence.

Stipendiary Wortman: The child is not fit to come

here. I have been told myself by Dr. Ross; and you know by common report that she is not in fit condition.

Mr. Smith: I have no information from the doctor himself on the subject and I know that there are more lies to the square inch being told about John Sullivan than about any other person living. I propose to put a stop to some of them if I can.

Stipendiary Wortman: Well, you have Mr. Sullivan right here, put him on the stand.

Mr. McCully: Yes, put him on and let him tell where he was from two o'clock on the afternoon preceding the Dutcher fire until 5 o'clock the next morning.

Mr. Smith: Never mind about that, Mr. McCully. I do not propose to do that just now. Wait until you have made out a case. I do not want to jeopardize the life of the child. All I ask is an adjournment of eight days so that Dr. Chandler, a reputable doctor, can give his opinion along with others.

Stipendiary Wortman: If you had intimated to me, Mr. Smith, that you wanted time to get some witness here to contradict something I would have granted it. But when you hang back and won't put your own man on, but want to put on that little girl when Dr. Ross says she is not fit, I have to say I cannot consent to an adjournment.

(*The Moncton Daily Times,* 27 November 1896)

Dr. Ross was subsequently called to confirm that she could not testify. Sullivan was formally committed for trial at the January term of the Supreme Court. The posting of bail was not permitted.

This third and final examination of the Meadow Brook tragedy began on January 12th, 1897, before Judge Hanington. Solicitor-General White, with F.A. McCully as the associate counsel, acted for the crown. Smith continued as Sullivan's defence. The trial was to last two weeks. At the beginning at least, Sullivan showed little concern that the result would be other than an acquittal. Again the same cast of witnesses were brought forward as had appeared at the inquest and preliminary examination. David Richard, the barber who had given Sullivan and his companions a shave only hours after the fire and had collected a month's advance from the accused, shared with the Court a rather puzzling fact. That same afternoon Sullivan had returned alone and asked for his money back, saying he was going on to Nova Scotia. This did not seem the expected behavior of a man who only a short while earlier had allegedly robbed the Dutcher household. Peter Foster, a neighbor who had been one of the first after Hugh Green to arrive at the scene of fire, reported that he had found $30.25 in a bureau drawer. Had a robbery actually occurred, or had the assailant simply missed this cache?

But other evidence that Sullivan had been involved in this frightful crime was more damning. The defence finally had its wish, but the result was not what had been hoped for. Accompanied by her nurses, Maggie Dutcher, now sufficiently recovered, was finally brought into the crowded court room. The large number of ladies present were disappointed that the child remained only long enough to testify, but were undoubtedly affected by the drama of the moment:

> The Solicitor General asked her if she knew it was wicked to tell lies.
>
> Answer: Yes.
>
> Have you gone to school?
>
> Yes.
>
> Do you know where good little girls go?
>
> Yes; to Heaven.
>
> Here the Judge asked: "Do you know you must tell the truth when you are sworn?"
>
> Yes.
>
> The Judge in a kind voice impressed upon Maggie the importance of being sure of what she said.
>
> *Examined by the Solicitor General:* Did you formerly live at Meadow Brook?
>
> Yes.
>
> Do you remember the last night you were there with your mamma and Harry?

Yes.

Did you sleep together?

Yes.

Who went to bed first?

Harry and I.

Were you awake when your mamma went to bed?

Yes.

Where did you sleep?

Harry at the back, mamma in front and me in the middle.

Were you awakened by a noise that night?

Yes.

What did you see?

There was a man in the room. Mamma said, "John, don't hit." The man had hold of mamma. He struck mamma two times. Momma laid back on the bed still. The man hit Harry. He then hit me and I cried. He hit me two times.

Solicitor General: Do you know who the man was?

Yes.

Who was it?

John Sullivan.

Do you see him in court?

The prisoner stood up.

Is that the man?

Maggie pointed to the prisoner with her finger and said: "That is him."

The prisoner was unmoved.

Maggie continued about as follows: That is the last I remember about Meadow Brook. I remember going to Moncton on the train. I do not remember being at Hugh Green's after that night. I was sick. I have been with Miss Croasdale a long time.

Cross-examined by Mr. Smith: I have been very sick. Miss Croasdale has been kind to me. I love her. I have seen my brothers since I was sick, but have not talked to them about what happened that night. I do not know where bad people go when they lie. We went to bed before dark that night. Harry and I went first and mamma came before we went to sleep. I woke up. It was daylight. I saw a man come into the room. I heard mamma say "stop." He hit her two times and she fell back on the bed. She did not fall on me. She never spoke again. The man lit the lamp. It was not dark. I knew John Sullivan well. He was often at our house. I liked him. He used to nurse me often. That night he hit me on the head, I cried. He hit me again. We had a dog. I did not see him that day nor the day before. I don't know what money momma had. I did not see John Sullivan take any. There was no person in the house that night when we went to bed. The dog never stayed in the house at nights. The doors were locked that night; I saw momma lock them. There were two other beds in the house — one in the big room and one in the little room.

To Solicitor General: I am sure mamma and Harry were struck two times. I did not see anything in John Sullivan's hand.

(*The St. John Globe,* 16 January 1897)

Smith's cross-examination confused the little girl and led to some contradictory statements. But in general her story held firm. The court recessed as she was led away.

The defence's accusation that Maggie had been coached as to what to say in court was vigorously denied by the Croasdale sisters, who had looked after the child. Indeed, the Solicitor-General charged, the accused's brother, Daniel, himself had "abused" some of the crown witnesses, and that threats against others had been made by members of the Sullivan family. Judge Hanington warned that if they were found guilty of this, they could be imprisoned for two years. The defendant was not helped by his family's behavior. Several days later his brother Charlie admitted to having recently choked William Dutcher for talking about the case.

Although not as dramatic as Maggie's testimony, the statements of other witnesses were not favorable to the accused. I.C.R. train hands repeated that none of them had seen Sullivan on any train coming into Moncton the night of the tragedy. George Warren, who met Sullivan in Saint John on Sunday afternoon, the 13th, reported the defendant confirmed what Jane Green had told the inquest. Sullivan admitted he had been at Mrs. Dutcher's drinking on the Thursday morning previous to the fire, and said his mother was anxious he should go on to his Uncle John's in Maine to avoid getting mixed up with the affair.

The defence opened its case calling, among others, Mrs. Sullivan. She once again testified that her son had come home on September 10th at 2 a.m. She did admit that she had coaxed him to go away so as to avoid appearing at the inquest. As she spoke, Sullivan was visibly moved. He shaded his face with his hands, and his eyes filled with tears.

Smith brought forward a sixteen-year-old youth, named McGary, who swore that on the night of the 10th he had been out after 11 p.m. looking for a bottle of liquor. Walking down by the wharf, he met a man and a woman. The man, he said, was Sullivan. Unfortunately for the defence, several days later the youth was recalled to the stand and admitted that he had been lying. He made up the story of seeing Sullivan, after he had been visited by the accused's brother.

Seeking to account for Sullivan's whereabouts the night of the fire, Smith introduced one Mary Ann Porrell to the court. She claimed that she had known Sullivan since childhood, and that on that fateful night at 9 p.m. he had come to her place of business, paying her a dollar and giving her a note for $15. This money was to be used for the support of a little child apparently fathered by Sullivan. The crown successfully attacked the credibility of this witness, and later showed that she too had been lying.

Sullivan, as he had not done earlier, finally took the stand himself. He testified that he had taken the train from Memramcook and arrived in Moncton about 8:15 p.m. that Thursday night. He met his sister and Miss Howell on the street subsequently. About

Hotel American, Moncton, New Brunswick. (PANB)

11 p.m. he followed two girls down the wharf track, although em-
phasizing that "nothing improper took place." Later he went home
quite sick from excessive drinking. He recounted his activities the
next day, differing at times from what other witnesses had testified.
He denied being at the Dutcher house early Thursday or Friday
morning. On Saturday his family urged him to leave town. After
obtaining a bottle of whiskey at the Hotel American he jumped
aboard a train to Sussex. As Sullivan completed his testimony, it
was learned that his mother had been taken seriously ill.

In his five-hour summation to the jury, the defence counsel argued for Sullivan's innocence, blaming the murder on tramps who
had been visiting through the countryside. As for Maggie's identi-
fication of Sullivan as the assailant, it was obvious to Smith that
she had been coached. In any case, no motive for the crime had
been established; robbery had not been proven. Solicitor-General
White's rebuttal was convincing to the Judge, who in his address
to the jury appeared decidedly against the prisoner. The jury
recessed at 1:00 p.m. After little more than an hour's deliberation
they returned with a guilty verdict. Sullivan was to be hung on
March 12th. His defence failed to appeal the sentence to the Su-

preme Court in Fredericton. Still protesting his innocence, Sullivan held some hope that a petition for clemency would be successful. Such was not to be the case.

From Dorchester jail's cell number eleven, where he was kept in solitary confinement as he awaited the execution of his sentence, Sullivan wrote a very revealing letter to a friend who resided at Calais. The condemned man's past — including travels around the world with the U.S. Navy and service as a bugler in the U.S. Cavalry in the war against the Apache — proved more colourful than perhaps many who had sat through the court room proceedings had realized:

> Dear Friend — There is no spot on earth that is so lonely and none so cheerless as a prison cell. Away from the world with its busy hum and business hustle is bad enough, but in a cell with grated prison door and an outside door which when closed makes my room look like a modern dungeon is even worse than an ordinary case of imprisonment. And then again I am not only incarcerated here for a certain period of time with hopes of regaining my liberty, but I am here for a few days only and I can count the hours when I will be taken from here and asked to say good bye to all the world and then mount the scaffold and die. Judge Hanington says so, the order must be obeyed. I am as innocent as a child unborn of the crime of murder, but what does that matter? The crown wanted a victim, and I was the only available man. Concerning my trial I have only to say that if public opinion ever took a hand in a public prosecution, it was in my particular case. However, as I write from behind these dark stone walls, I only do so to let the public know that I am not satisfied with the manner in which the criminal law of Canada is administered in this country. I make this complaint, as one who has been tried and found guilty of murder in the Supreme Court of Westmorland county. My complaint will not alter the present state of affairs, but it will go down to future generations as a sort of protest

against the mock trial system which is such a curse to our country at the present time . . . .

I was born in Westmorland county in 1860, and when quite young I went to school to Mr. Friel, father of James Friel, barrister at Dorchester. I got a common school education, but I regret to say that I did not put my services to any profitable use. I went to work in a saw mill, after which I went on the I.C.R. as a section hand, but grew tired of the business and again went milling. I soon took a notion to go railroading again, and got employment as a brakeman, but owing to the dull times I went to the State of Maine, where I worked for over a year in the saw mills, but wanting to see more of the world I shipped on board the *Anna S. Brown*, then commanded by Captain McGrath of St. Stephen. The *Anna Brown* was bound for Newark, N.J. When I reached my destination I shipped in the United State navy in the ship Boston, and made two voyages almost around the world, stopping in all the principal cities in the world. When I arrived back in New York I was sent on board of a torpedo boat as deckhand, which position I held for six months, when I was promoted to pilot of the torpedo boat, *David Bushnell*, then a new boat for the engineers.

After some time I grew tired of harbor life and just then the Apache Indians broke out and went on the warpath in Arizona, and I was sent to Arizona with some others, attached to the Second Cavalry, I being reserved as a bugler and courier. I had quite a varied experience and witnessed a great deal of brutality and genuine butchery. I stuck to the cavalry till the Indians were subdued and returned to their respective reservations. Then we were sent back to New York, where I gave up the trumpet and shipped on board of one of the Anchor line boats running between New York and England. I made two voyages, after which I shipped on a small steamer named the *Dundee*, running between England and the

East Indies and China. I made four voyages in her, when I was taken ill with the fever and sent to the hospital. After my recovery I returned to my home, and being advised by my parents to reside in Canada, I went to work in the mills in Westmorland county and in Nova Scotia, and have recommendations in my possession from all the firms with whom I have ever been employed; and now I would like to say that in all my travels in the different foreign countries where I have gone, I never saw the inside of a prison cell and was entirely unknown to the officers of the law until I was arrested at Calais, Me., on a charge of being implicated in the Meadow Brook tragedy.

Since my arrest I have not asked for public sympathy, nor have I any idea of doing so now. Moreover, I know that the whole force of public opinion has set in against me and that it militated against me at my trial, and that even the judge who presided over the court was prejudiced against me . . . . I freely forgive all my enemies, and hope that God in His great goodness will forgive them also. I am called upon to offer up my life on the scaffold on the charge of murder. That is false and has no foundation in fact or in law. I feel sorry to leave behind me in disgrace an aged father and a loving mother, whose old heart is sore on account of her erring son. My dear sisters whom I love with all my heart will have to bear all the disgrace that a vagabond brother has brought upon them. God bless and keep my sisters, and make them able to bear the name of their brother without murmuring too much, and

My Poor Mother,
"Weep, my poor old mother, weep,
Let tears fall fast and free;
They will help to ease your troubled heart
Of woe and agony.
Weep for the loss of your poor son,

Whom you will see no more.
He's bound down in iron fetters strong
And his heart with grief is sore."
.... I will now say good-bye to all the people.

Sincerely yours,
John E. Sullivan.
Dorchester Jail

(The St. John Globe, 24 February 1897)

Because he had served in the U.S. Army, Washington apparently made some inquiries regarding Sullivan's fate. The Cabinet in Ottawa refused to commute his sentence; nor at the same time were they inclined to show mercy toward an Indian convicted of killing a sergeant of the Northwest Mounted Police. The prison chaplain, Father Cormier — who had also ministered to Buck in his last days several years earlier — broke the news to Sullivan, who showed neither surprise nor concern: "Father, do you think for a moment you are breaking any sad news to me. It is nothing more than I expected" *(The St. John Globe,* 6 March 1897).

In the days preceding the execution Sullivan spent his time reading books. He seemed prepared to die, and to one reporter who visited him showed surprising composure:

"Well, I've only a short time to live now, but I've nothing to fear." "Nothing to fear?" queried the reporter, "No, nothing," replied Sullivan "nothing. I've faced death a hundred times and I'm not going to flinch now."

"But this is sure death."

"I know, but I will face it bravely, I am not afraid to die. The noise I hear does not worry me. I slept as well last night as I ever did in my life. I have no statement to make other than what I have told you. Nothing I can say will make any difference now."

(The St. John Globe, 10 March 1897)

Ironically, the same hangman — Radcliffe — who effected Buck's final fate was enlisted for the execution. As he arrived from Toronto, lumber was brought to the jail to erect the scaffold in the same manner as had been done several years earlier. From his cell

Sullivan could hear the carpenters at work. But even this did not appear to distress him. He and Father Cormier walked up and down the corridor of the jail. The chaplain found him resigned to his fate: "He seems to realize his fate fully, but has faith that he will receive divine pardon for his sins. He pays the strictest attention to my words and his manner pleases me greatly. I fully believe Sullivan is sincerely penitent and is in a fit state of mind to go before his God" (*The St. John Globe,* 11 March 1897).

The day before the execution, Sullivan was shaved by one of the other prisoners. He delayed breakfast until he received communion from Father Roy, Superior of St. Joseph's College, who spent the morning with the condemned man. Sullivan showed no fear of death nor a willingness to confess:

"Why, it is a lucky thing for me in one way. I might have met death suddenly when I had no thoughts of God; now it is different. I am prepared and can face the future without flinching. There is no statement I can make other than what I have said."

Asked if he would simply say whether he was guilty or innocent, Sullivan replied, "I would not answer that question if my liberty was given me for it. I am condemned and will say nothing of that kind. You may deny any stories about any confessions or stories of my career. They are false."

Receiving a handful of cigars from a friend, Sullivan said with a smile: "There are more here than I can smoke while I live, I guess." To the sheriff he said: "You and Mr. Bowes have used me well. You must give me a good breakfast tomorrow." "Anything you want you can have, John," replied the sheriff.

(*The St. John Globe,* 11 March 1897)

Sullivan's family arrived from Moncton to spend the last afternoon with him. His mother was still too ill to travel, however. The accused's father only decided to come at the last moment. The elder Sullivan continued to advance to the end his son's innocence. Only the prisoner's brothers, Dan and Charlie, remained as the other members of the family bade good-bye, returning home on the late afternoon train. An awkward visit was paid as well by the executioner. Radcliffe wished to take note of the condemned man's size and weight to ensure an efficient hanging. Sullivan greeted the hangman without hostility:

> He at once stepped up to him and shook him by the hand, gazing calmly at him, not flinching in the least from the man whose duty it was in a few hours to launch him into eternity. "Well, John, you know who I am; I am sorry for you, but cannot help you," he said in soft kindly tones. "I am only the instrument of the law." "I know," Sullivan replied, "you can't help it. After all it might as well be you as anyone else. I was really glad when I heard you were to do it. I was afraid the sheriff might undertake it and he is old and fussy, and there might have been a bungle that would have caused me torture. I have no fear of that now."
>
> (*The St. John Globe,* 12 March 1897)

Sullivan ate well his last night, sampling some cake, coffee, toast and preserves. The chaplain remained with him until 10. The prisoner would not let the priest stay longer; he said he must have sleep so as to have strength in the morning. Father Cormier expressed little doubt of Sullivan's innocence:

> That man is not a criminal. He has not the nature of a criminal. During all the time I have been with him I never heard him say a harsh word about anyone. He is thoughtful and kind and his is not the nature of a man who would commit a cruel murder. I cannot and will not believe that he committed such a crime as the circumstantial evidence against him showed. So far he has said nothing except at the sacramental confession. What he said there is between himself and God. He said nothing to me about confessing, but I gather from the few things he said, and a few little incidents, that if he had pleaded guilty to the crime just as it really happened, and not listened to the bad advice of friends, he would have got off with a few

years in the penitentiary. I believe if he were allowed to go free now he would become a remarkably good citizen. So strongly do I feel that if such a thing were possible I would become his bondsman even with my life.

(The St. John Globe, 12 March 1897)

Sullivan slept soundly, rising after five and partaking of a light breakfast. He said he slept well and felt well. To Jailer Bowles he indicated this was the happiest morning of his life. Father Cormier and Father Roy arrived to give him the sacrament. Several ladies dressed in mourning arrived to console him. One such visitor, a Protestant, had earlier caused some concern among the priests lest she "interfere with" the prisoner's religion. The two brothers were admitted to say their final farewells. Sullivan urged Charlie to take warning by his fate and lead a good life.

At 7:35 a.m. the noose was placed around Sullivan's neck. Between fifty and sixty persons witnessed the execution. The younger brother fainted as he heard the dull thud of the drop weight as it fell in a bed of sawdust. Two minutes later Sullivan was pronounced dead. The scaffold was cleared, and an inquest, as the law demanded, was quickly held. The body was taken to the Catholic chapel where Father Cormier conducted the services. The condemned man was buried not far from Buck's grave in the Catholic cemetery.

The mystery of Sullivan's real guilt or innocence, or of whether anyone else was involved in the crime, remained as the casket was lowered into the ground. The closest Sullivan came to a confession was with some brief words to the chaplain in the final days: "Father, I will take the whole blame myself. I will not bring shame upon anyone else, or implicate anyone." Sullivan had left a letter for the priest to open after the execution. It was full of beautiful thoughts, the chaplain said, and he would treasure it highly . . . .

"TIRED OF THIS WORLD"

The number of recorded cases of (including attempted) suicide in Charlottetown and in other Maritime urban communities during the late nineteenth century was quite small. Because of the stigma attached to the act of self-destruction, this is not surprising; the actual number may have been greater but was concealed by family members and others anxious to protect their standing in the community.

In some cases where the motive was unknown, suicide appeared as an inexplicable and irrational act, a sudden and dramatic departure from the routines of daily life. In late October, 1878, a farmer named Patrick McQuaid, residing at Lot 30, awoke at 1 a.m. on a Sunday morning. Getting out of bed, he told his wife he wanted to shave and asked for his razor. The wife felt something odd about this. Pretending to help her husband look for the razor she hid it. McQuaid gave up looking, returned to bed, and slept the remainder of the night. Rising at his usual hour the next morning, he went out to the yard. Before his wife could stop him, he took hold of an axe and cut his throat from ear to ear, and died (*The Daily Examiner,* 22 October 1878).

Rather than leave such an act unexplained, suicide was wont to be attributed to a temporary (or more permanent) mental aberration. Insanity, melancholy, loss of a desire to live, were correctly or incorrectly cited as the cause for this most irrevocable act:

A case of attempted suicide was reported from St. Peter's Road, this forenoon. A servant girl in the employ of Mr. John Ferguson, was left alone in the house attending to her duties when Mr. Ferguson and the farm hands went to work. She was apparently in cheerful spirits and was occupied at washing the breakfast dishes when they left. Twenty minutes after their departure, one of the hands returned and found her almost lifeless body suspended by a rope to a beam in the workshop. He cut it down and then ran to the field in which Mr. Ferguson was at work, and informed him of the occurrence. Mr. Ferguson returned to the house, and seeing symptoms of life in the body, came to the city for medical aid. But we learn he could not get any. One doctor informed Mr. Ferguson, that if the girl was alive, she was all right, and if she was dead he would be no help to her. The unfortunate girl's name is Small. Her parents reside a short distance from Mr. Ferguson's residence. We learn that this Miss Small, last July, while laboring under a fit of insanity, wandered from Mr. Ferguson's residence, and was found by the neighbours who turned out in full force to search for her, in the vicinity of Crosby's Creek. She was completely exhausted when found, and totally unconscious of her wanderings. Since July she informed her mother that she had been at one time seized with a similar fit, but it was not so bad as the first. It is likely that while laboring under a fit of mental depression, that she attempted to end her life.

(*The Daily Examiner*, 23 October 1880)

The "mental aberration" that supposedly resulted in the suicide could itself be "traced" to a significant change in health or personal circumstances, as illustrated in the rather sad case of one Mrs. Cross, the sixty-year-old wife of a saddler on Grafton St.:

... Three months ago she fell on a sidewalk and broke one of her legs, and was confined to her bed until three weeks ago. Shortly after she began to move about, she began to show signs of mental aberration. She would rarely talk with any person, but when she would she remarked she was tired of this world and wished she were out of it ....

(*The Daily Examiner*, 11 April 1887)

Her exit was a rather violent one. One day she seized a poker from the stove and thrust it down her throat. A doctor was summoned. He asked her why she had done this. She repeated that she was tired of life and wanted to leave the world. Mrs. Cross and her husband had been hard drinkers; indeed liquor was said to be the cause of their "reduced circumstances."

Temperance advocates could perhaps derive some moral lesson from this; suicide itself, when it was preceded by a dramatic change in social status, seemed equally understandable. Such occurred in the case of an attempted suicide by John Jackson, a "well-known resident of Douglass Street." Jackson's trade was that of a cooper, but he had been out of work for some time. Unemployment did not sit well with him; becoming despondent, he fell ill. Despite an apparently brief recovery, he decided one Monday to end it all. Waiting until his wife and servant girl had left the house, he took a razor to his upstairs bedroom. Lifting the razor to his throat he inflicted a severe gash from the bottom of his right ear to the centre of his throat. Not satisfied with the injury, he made an additional cut there. Although bleeding profusely, he was saved by the quick action of a doctor summoned by the servant girl who had returned to the house. Jackson's aim was faulty; missing a major artery, he was still fortunate to survive. That unemployment seemed the cause of such a radical action was apparent after taking note of his normal state:

> Jackson is a big, stout, jolly-looking person, about 35 years of age, and from appearances the last man that one would suspect of being about to commit suicide. He was well known as a comedian and vocalist, being a frequent performer at variety entertainments, and the leading spirit in several minstrel troupes organized in this city the past five years. During the past two years, however, he has at times been gloomy and despondent, and it was during one of these fits . . . that he made the attempt at self-destruction.
>
> (*The Daily Examiner*, 22 June 1886)

Aside from a change in social status, suicide also appeared a viable alternative to the dispossessed. The transients, the rootless, at least at some point, may have found little else to shield them:

On Queen's Wharf, last evening, a watchman on one of the vessels perceived a woman walking to and fro. In her arms she carried a child snugly wrapped up in a shawl. Her movements excited his suspicion, and in the darkness he drew near in order to detect her intentions. Once she walked to one side of the wharf and looked over, thence she crossed to the opposite side and examined the waters below. Again turning she walked to the head and leaned over it a few moments apparently contemplating suicide, or the drowning of her child. The watchman called to and then approached her. She did not speak but a few indistinct words. He, thinking she was unsafe alone, gave her in charge of the police. Her name is Davis. She came from Boston last summer, and has since been tramping through the country, depending on the charity of the people. Having no friends in the city, or no money, she could not get shelter or food, and she wandered to the wharf in a melancholy frame of mind, with, if we may judge, serious intentions. Her child — fifteen months old — was taken in charge by M. Merchant, watchman, and the Magistrate will endeavor to have her admitted to the Government Poor House.

(*The Daily Examiner,* 15 December 1881)

Strangers visited Charlottetown. Some brought with them "world-views" not congruent with those held locally. This clash was underscored in the attempted suicide of a 27-year-old American sailor, named Winsloe Hawes, in late July, 1878. He was a resident of Wellford, Massachusetts, where he had left a wife and family. He had just recently arrived at Charlottetown in the hope of getting on a vessel bound for an American port. He appeared one evening at the Apothecaries Hall and purchased two ounces of laudanum from Charles Hughes. Two hours later Hawes returned to the store and asked Hughes how much laudanum made a full dose. After Hughes told him, the American admitted to having drank the two ounces he had earlier purchased. Leaving the store, he went down Queen Street. Alarmed, Hughes notified the City Marshal, who found Hawes staggering on Steam Navigation Wharf. After initially refusing to answer any questions, he admitted to having swallowed the poison. He then showed the Marshal the bottle. The label had been removed, however, for a seemingly altruistic reason: "He expected that the poison would kill him; the bottle would then be found on his person, the label would show whom he got it from; the person who gave it to him would get into trouble, and he did not want any person to get into trouble about him" (*The Daily Examiner,* 27 July 1878). The Marshal arrested and took him to the Station. An emetic was dispensed, which saved the life of this would-be suicide. Both the Marshal and Magistrate, as would most Charlottetowners at the time, found the explanation given for self-destruction rather abstruse:

> When asked by the Marshal what reason he had for doing away with his life, he said he did not believe there was a hell except this earth, and he was on it long enough. When asked the same question by the Stipendiary Magistrate, he said he thought he might as well commit suicide; he was tired of this life, and he wanted to die. He had no idea that it was against the law to commit suicide; had he known it was against the law he would not attempt to do it in this country. The Magistrate said: "Was it not God gave you your life; and what right have you to do away with it?" He replied that God never told him anything to the contrary. He thought he had a perfect right to take it away. Hawes is a Free Thinker, belongs to the Congregationalist religion, and is a bright specimen of the free thinking engendered by the Republican institutions across the border.
>
> (*The Daily Examiner,* 27 July 1878)

Despair motivated suicide. But the participants of this and other illegal acts cogently demonstrated that not all were as strongly attached to the values and norms of the community as were supposedly the "respectable" citizenry.

Halifax, too, saw the drama of suicide. The ready availability of "Rough on Rats," a form of arsenic, was vigorously condemned. As in Charlottetown, the motives for its use or of that other forms of self-destruction were unsettling.

THE ABSENT ARTILLERYMAN

George Davies was a young recruit from England, serving as a royal artilleryman at Fort Clarence, on the other side of the Halifax harbor. Of quiet demeanor, abstinent, and obedient to his superiors, one day in late August, 1884, he obtained a short leave of absence but did not return. Instead, it was later reported, he took to drink, and formed a liaison with a young woman named Young. The girl's family had left a year or more earlier also from England, and settled in Dartmouth. Her mother was a respectable woman, who obtained work at the Mount Hope asylum. The daughter was employed as a domestic servant in the family of Mr. Doeg, manager of the Woodside refinery, and resident of Dartmouth. Although her work was satisfactory, her mother had found her a rather truculent teenager. Her headstrong ways continued as she made the acquaintance of Gunner Davies. The two were secretly married, and after the daughter left her employ, they camped in the woods nearby. Following a period of heavy drinking, the couple resolved to end their lives together. The girl purchased a package of "Rough on Rats," with the plan that they would both partake. Davies consumed his share between two biscuits, and washed it down with lemonade. These were obtained at the Sandy Cove bathing house. The girl threw away her share of the package. Shortly afterwards her husband became quite sick. An alarm was sounded. Word was sent to Fort Clarence. The sergeant in charge, with others from the garrison, rushed to the beach where the poisoned man was lying. A crowd congregated around him. The girl was found playfully throwing pieces of wood and matches at her stricken partner, apparently oblivious to his condition. Davies was taken to the Mount Hope asylum where an anemic was administered. He requested that he be transferred to the military hospital to die, but did not want to go back to the fort. Nothing could be done for him there. The following morning he died. His reluctance to return to the garrison puzzled authorities. His previous stature as an exemplary soldier meant that his brief absence would not have drawn other than a mild punishment. Equally anomalous was the girl's apparent unconcern for her companion's fate (*The Halifax Morning Herald,* 26 August 1884).

THE MELANCHOLY WIFE

A Halifax woman thought she had found a forgiving husband in 1881. Sadie Innis married Corporal Mansfield of the Ordinance Store Corps when she was 24 years old. That she had not yet legally severed the bond to her first husband, a private of one of the regiments previously stationed there, did not appear to be of concern to her new spouse. Their domestic life appeared peaceful for the next three years, until the Corporal began to abuse her, and her past was resurrected. In September, 1884, Sadie received an anonymous letter, from "A Friend," informing her that in three days a warrant would be issued for her arrest as a bigamist, and advising her to leave at once for the States. She showed the letter to her husband, who told her she would have to go at once. She wished to remain, to face whatever the consequences. Mansfield would not hear of this. Giving her only a little money, he put her on the train for Somerville, Massachusetts. There she obtained lodging at the residence of Mrs. Robert Thompson, where she remained for two weeks, paying board the first week and earning her keep as a domestic the second. She wrote her husband, urging that he send enough money for her return to Halifax. He refused, and wrote a letter threatening her if she should come back. Turning to her sister, she was able to obtain sufficient funds to purchase a ticket home. After arriving by boat, she stayed with her sister. She contacted her husband, who promised that he would arrange to pay for her board in Halifax. Mansfield refused to have anything more to do with her. One Saturday afternoon shortly thereafter she left her sister's house, saying she was going to purchase some clothes. Returning within hours, she lay down on the mat in front of the stove, complaining of feeling ill. Later on she got up and went to bed. Her condition worsened through the night. Word was sent to her husband to come at once if he wished to see his wife alive. He did not relent. Several hours later she died. A doctor was summoned, but it was too late.

Before Sadie died, she told her sister that there was a letter in her box which she wished her husband to receive. He refused to read it. After the funeral the sister opened it:

Steve — Life is nothing to me without you, so I am going to end it, but I forgive you all at this my last moment .... Good by, I hope God will forgive me,

Sadie.

The letter was not all she found. While putting away some of Sadie's clothing a box of poison — "Rough on Rats" — dropped out of a pocket. The sister informed Mansfield about the poison. He told her not to mind it (*The Halifax Morning Herald*, 10 December 1884).

A FATEFUL STAY AT THE QUEEN

The tragedy of suicide was heightened when its motives could only be suspected, as occurred in the case of Mrs. Robert Walford, who shot herself through the heart in Halifax in July of 1887.

Mrs. Sadie Walford was the wife of a well-known New York shipping broker, who had done considerable business with many Nova Scotian ship owners. She was born in England and had married her husband, a Southerner, while still relatively young. At the time of her death she had two daughters, Ada, aged eleven and Alice, aged thirteen. The family's permanent residence was in Brooklyn. In 1882, Mrs. Walford, her husband and two children took a summer tour of Nova Scotia, and visited Halifax, Chester, Liverpool, and other communities, where they made a number of acquaintances. Four years later Mrs. Walford returned alone to Halifax, spending the summer and early fall there at the home of some friends on Pleasant Street and having a fairly active social life. In November 1886, she had arranged to return to her family in New York, but suddenly changed her mind and instead went to Chester, Nova Scotia, where she stayed for the winter. In March

The Queen Hotel, Halifax, Nova Scotia, 1887. (PANS)

she once again came to Halifax, took accommodation for four days at the Queen Hotel, and then departed supposedly for home. She never left the city; the next two months or more she resided at another hotel or boarding house. On June 13th, 1887, she called at the Queen, inquiring if she could remain there for several weeks. The proprietor, Mr. Sheraton, indicated that because of the large number of summer travellers expected the Hotel could not take in permanent boarders. She insisted, and he relented, giving her room No. 69.

She was an appealing guest. Apparently she had been blessed with musical talents. Not only was she a fine pianist, she was an excellent vocalist and entertained the other guests in the parlor. There were several rather puzzling aspects of her stay in the Queen. She had registered under the name of Mrs. J.H. Walston, New York, and received no correspondence at all from her husband in New York. Although she went out driving on several occasions and had frequent contact with several gentlemen in Halifax, she did not call on some of the close friends she had made during her long visit there the previous summer.

At the end of June she asked the Queen's proprietor for her bill, and paid what was owed to that point. On the night of June 30th she had her tea sent to her room. At approximately ten o'clock, two guests — Wellington Chase, an artist and portrait painter, and William Lind, a commercial traveller from Montreal — occupying adjoining rooms heard the sounds of a revolver fired and of groans in Mrs. Walford's room. They rushed out to the hallway, and alerted the porter and proprietor. Together they went to Room No. 69. Sheraton knocked. There was no answer. He looked through the transom and as he smelled powder, sensed that something was wrong. The door was unlocked. As they entered, they saw Mrs. Walford, still in her nightdress, reclining on an easy chair. Her right hand tightly grasped a large revolver. The tea stood on a tray undisturbed. On a bureau nearby lay an empty envelope, addressed to Mr. Robert Walford, 51 South Street, New York. Sheraton immediately called for a doctor, but it was apparent it was too late. Lind took the woman's left hand to feel her pulse. She gasped loudly several times, and died in his arms after only a few minutes. The Coroner was summoned to take charge of the body and arrange for an inquest.

Among Mrs. Walford's effects in her room was found a trunk containing valuable jewelry and clothing. In addition, there were many letters from her husband over a period of years, but none dated within the previous six months. Her effects included a tincture of digitalis, apparently used for possible heart trouble, a flask of brandy, photographs of herself and her two children, several novels (*Dead Men's Shoes*, *The Guilty River*), and evidence that she had taken morphine.

The authorities immediately advised her husband in New York of her death. A "cold-hearted" telegraph was received in response:

Fear insanity. You take charge of everything. Presume weather necessitates immediate interment, which please attend to as I cannot get on in time. Again my partner's wife is very ill. He is away from city. Forward funds tomorrow.

(Sgd.) R.M.G. Walford.

That the dead woman and her husband had been estranged for some time was apparent. Her neighbors in New York later recalled the transformation in Sadie from a vivacious newlywed to a woman, after several years of marriage, marked by extreme sadness. Before her trip to Nova Scotia, she had confided to a friend that she was in deep trouble, adding without explanation, "And they say it is my fault. It won't last long, however." The friend urged Sadie to do nothing rash, reminding her that she had two children who needed care and should not be neglected. "I will always remember them," she responded, "and I have prepared my jewelry so that they may divide it between them and wear it." The suspicion was that she might have been planning suicide long before she reached Nova Scotia. A Halifax bookkeeper, who had a long acquaintance with her family and visited them in Brooklyn, described her as a very genial lady, but one easily elated or depressed.

It appears her husband never returned to Halifax to visit her grave (*The Halifax Morning Herald,* 1 July 1887; 2 July 1887; 7 July 1887).

Vagrants and Tramps

The poor were part of Charlottetown's "underclass," as they were in other Maritime urban communities of the late nineteenth century. In early February, 1880, the Women's Temperance Union and Benevolent Society opened a soup kitchen for the winter. Donations, including clothing, were requested from the public. That the demands for assistance were pressing notwithstanding, the Society wished to ensure that only the "worthy poor" were aided: "In order to distribute judiciously, only those will be relieved who identify themselves with the Society, which will enable the committee to look particularly into each case" (*The Daily Examiner,* 2 February 1880).

The deserving should be helped; but in the community's view, they must help themselves. The report of the Treasurer of the Central Committee for the Relief of the Worthy Poor for the last week in January was applauded for this reason. One hundred of the unemployed, for a total payment of between $80 and $90, were put to work in the different woods yards and in breaking stone. As evidence of their "worthiness," it was confidently reported, the men preferred to work for a wage than to receive a "gratuity."

Charlottetown's streets, however, were visited by those unable through their own efforts to change their rather hopeless plight. Some sought protection overnight in the police station. Others the police themselves brought in, at times on a charge of vagrancy, to provide temporary shelter:

> John Ferguson, vagrant, took refuge in the lock-up last
> night, and was discharged today. It is a pity that authori-

rities should allow this helpless invalid to loiter about the city. He is a sickening sight to all who pass him. Cannot something be done to take him off the streets?

(The Daily Examiner, 11 October 1879)

An unfortunate girl, some 16 yrs. of age, who has evidently "loved not wisely," was found by the police wandering about the streets seeking shelter from the bitter cold and finding none, at 2 o'clock on Sunday morning. She was taken to the station and warned; thence to jail, from which she was discharged this morning. The poor girl said she had travelled all the way from Georgetown on foot.

(The Daily Examiner, 15 December 1879)

An old vagrant named Alex McLaren sought refuge at the Police Station last night. He appeared at Court this morning and it was decided to get him admission to the Poor House. We are informed that McLaren has $70 in bank, and while he hoards his cash he passes through the country begging, suffering at times exposure and starvation.

(The Daily Examiner, 17 November 1880)

A sad case was presented at the Stipendiary Magistrate's Court this forenoon. An old negro, named James Potter, lame, and a "subject of falling sickness," appeared as a vagrant. He had been forsaken by his friends and cast out upon the street. Food or shelter he could not obtain and the police, in order that he might not perish on the street, were obliged to arrest him as a vagrant. The Magistrate ordered that he be confined to jail for a fortnight, during which time application will be made for admission to the Poor House.

(The Daily Examiner, 31 October 1881).

At one o'clock a young woman named Mary Munroe was arrested while wandering through the streets with a child in her arms. She was homeless and without means. She was taken before the Stipendiary Magistrate this morning, but he, being unable to render her any official assistance, ordered that she be discharged from custody.

(*The Daily Examiner,* 10 November 1882)

... A vagrant woman, with a bright little child in her arms, was charged with lying out at nights without protection; but several charitable ladies having volunteered to look after her the charge was withdrawn.

(*The Daily Examiner,* 5 July 1884)

While cases such as these elicited some, although, as the above suggest, not universal, sympathy, particular condemnation was reserved for those classified as "the undeserving poor" — the tramps, the professional beggars, the able-bodied perceived as more willing to accept charity than menial labor. This distinction between the "worthy" and "undeserving" poor was not unique to Charlottetown, of course, but reflected a more general theme, the echoes of which were evident throughout nineteenth-century urban Canada. That the condition of poverty appeared a product more of a character defect than of any failure in the urban economy was substantiated for the "respectable" by the cases of the undeserving they encountered:

Yesterday a thorough-bred tramp sauntered to the house of one of our townsmen. Wishing to see the master of the house, and being gratified to that extent, the tramp asked for a few cents. There was an aroma of bad Jamaica in the surrounding air, and an anxious arid aspect on the lips of the tramp. "I possess a potatoe patch," said the gentleman, "and it needs weeding; go do that and I will repay you." But the tramp replied, "I likes a gentleman to give a fellow a few cents without working for it." Finding the gentleman firm in his resolve, the tramp took his departure. Presently he appeared again on the scene and wished to know if it would be all the same to the matter if another fellow did the work or helped him, while [the] tramp took the money. He was answered in the negative. Then, with blasted hopes and dolorous looks, he tramped off centless, but, we fancy, with sounder sense than he had before.

(*The Daily Examiner,* 5 July 1881)

The tramp ascended the front steps, and after taking the precaution to read the doorplate, rang the bell with a free and easy confidence born of previous successes. The door was opened by a woman, as the tramp had anticipated. "Is Mr. Brown in?" he asked. The woman took an inventory of his face and clothing, and replied sharply, "No, Mr. Brown isn't in; *Mrs.* Brown *is.* I've just sent Brown for a cent's worth of yeast; when he comes back he'll have to put out the line and hang out the wash, then I shall send him out with the baby, and after that he will have his sweeping and dusting to do. No, you can't see Brown today and 'twouldn't make any difference if you could. I attend to business here." The tramp guessed he'd mistaken the house, and Mrs. Brown, as she slammed the door, said she reckoned he had. Then the tramp shuffled away from the house in search of another where the women were not so self-poised and high spirited.

(*The Daily Examiner,* 26 June 1882)

Last night a strong, healthy young man about eighteen years old, entered the police station and after informing the officer in charge that he had no place to go, asked for protection for the night. The officer granted his request, and the young man, after picking out a soft spot on one of the seats, stretched himself for the night. This morning, after straightening out some of the kinks in his hair, and giving his face a "surprise party" in the shape of a mild dose of water, he started over to the Magistrate's Courtroom, accompanied by a guard of honour in the person of a stalwart officer. After a brief wait His Honour arrived, and the Marshall lost no time about making the two better acquainted. After the young man's case had been explained to His Honour, he sentenced him to one month's imprisonment as a common vagrant. The young man "went down smiling." He is one of several able-bodied fellows who spend their time during the summer eating wherever and whatever they can, and sleeping in the open air at night, and about this time each year manage to get sent down to jail for vagrancy. It's a great pity there's not some real hard work for those jail birds to do during their incarceration.

(The Daily Examiner, 9 November 1887)

The Magistrate did seek to follow this advice. Vagrants were not infrequently sentenced to a term "with hard labor," although it is not evident whether the latter was fully effected. Another alternative, one that was also resorted to, was to give the convicted vagrant 24 hours to leave the city. This would free the community from supporting the "shiftless," ensuring that they kept on the move at least to the next "town of call."

Vagrancy was also a charge lodged against Charlottetown's youths found wandering the streets late at night. In part this was an effort to control street corner loafing. It also reflected the desire to deal with troublesome youths who were engaged in other types of mischief and illegal behavior. Not uncommonly, youthful vagrants were also found to be involved in theft, assault, and disturbance of the peace:

Michael Purcell appeared for assaulting his father. The assault was in no way serious; but as Michael is a notorious vagrant, the Magistrate sentenced him to six months' imprisonment for vagrancy . . . .

(The Daily Examiner, 5 November 1879)

Two young vagrants, named McDonald and White were arrested by the police today. They have been implicated in several petty larcenies of late, and an enquiry into the charges laid against them will be made tomorrow. . . .

(The Daily Examiner, 8 March 1880)

Three of a gang of east end vagrants were disposed of, one being fined $20 or 30 days, for assaulting a companion with a knife during a drunken brawl, another was sentenced to one month's imprisonment, and the third was given 24 hours to leave the City . . . .

(The Daily Examiner, 10 May 1886)

Between eleven and twelve o'clock yesterday forenoon two boys, named Amrose and Francis Doyle, twelve or thirteen years of age, effected an entrance into the store of Messrs. Dorsey, Goff & Co., through a small window in the rear of the building. Mr. Joseph A. Macdonald noticed the leg of one of the boys as he was disappearing inside the store. He immediately notified the police, but on their arrival they discovered that the window through which the boys had entered was not sufficiently large to allow them to pass in, so they were forced to remain outside guarding the aperture while the key of the store was forthcoming. On the arrival of the key the door was opened, and a search instituted for the youthful desperadoes. After a short search one was found hidden under a packing case, and the other stowed away among the folds of a roll of leather. They were immediately searched but nothing was found on them, after which they were taken to the police station, and this morning arraigned before the Stipendiary Magistrate and sentenced to six months for vagrancy.

(The Daily Examiner, 17 May 1886)

As the above suggests, there was greater latitude for a conviction with a charge of vagrancy than with more serious offences. If the latter could not be sufficiently proven, the police and Court could resort to classifying the unruly youths as vagrants and then imposing a suitable sentence. The charge of vagrancy could, therefore, be lodged for a variety of motives — as earlier noted, to justify temporary shelter for the dispossessed, but also to control and punish delinquent youths.

Beier in his study of sixteenth- and seventeenth-century vagrancy in England indicates that vagrants were seen as "masterless men," as threats to social order:

> The masterless man represented mutability, when those in power longed for stability. He stood for poverty, which seemed to threaten their social and political dominance. Fundamentally, in prescribing that the vagrant be employed, governments were preoccupied with a problem of disorder.
>
> (A.L.Beier, *Masterless Men: The Vagrancy Problem in England, 1560-1650* [London: Methuen, 1987], 9-10)

Such also appeared to be the case in the late nineteenth-century Maritimes. The "undeserving poor" who wandered the streets were viewed as a potential challenge to a community's social harmony. This was underscored for Charlottetowners in rather dramatic fashion, in 1884, by the activities of a man labelled "the tramp." Repeatedly he entered residences at night, even while the occupants were asleep. His objective was not necessarily theft; he had a penchant for visiting the rooms of women and servant girls:

> A tramp entered the residence of Mr. Wm. Peardon, corner Great George and Fitzroy streets, through a window, on Monday night, and passed into Mrs. Peardon's bedroom. He passed his cold hand on Mrs. Peardon and she becoming alarmed, called her husband. The tramp beat a hasty retreat without being observed . . . .
>
> (*The Daily Examiner,* 24 September 1884)

It is not evident that he actually committed any assaults. Nonetheless, incidents such as these created some level of hysteria for a brief time in the community. Strident calls for his capture and punishment were accompanied by threats to retaliate without the sanction of the law:

Sir, — The infernal villain who has for some time past terrorized our citizens with his noctural visits, cannot go much longer unpunished. Last night, or rather about one o'clock this morning, he entered the residence of a prominent citizen, residing on King Square, gaining ingress through one of the upper windows which happened to be unfastened. One of the family being awake, heard a noise, like a heavy thud, which was succeeded by the falling of some heavy article. An alarm was at once given, and the cowardly tramp made his exit without being identified. It is generally understood that by killing a person under such circumstances it is constituted murder.

Such is not the case. If you find in your dwelling, at an unreasonable hour, any suspicious individual, you would, by shooting him, be guilty only of manslaughter; and in cases similar to the above, we believe it would be justifiable.

A feeling of dread has come over our people, and the sooner summary measures are resorted to in ridding the community of this nuisance the better. The surest medicine would be a few pills made of out the hardest lead.

Lynch

(The Daily Examiner, 4 September 1884)

Rumours and gossip circulated widely as to the identity of "the tramp." Suspicion focused on one J.W. Whitman, a veterinary surgeon, who because of his occupation made frequent jaunts from community to community. This was not the type of mobility characteristic of the itinerant underclass. Certainly Whitman himself strenuously rejected the accusation:

Sir, — . . . On Wednesday last, I received a despatch from Jas. E. Birch, of Alberton, to attend a sick horse. So I took the train and arrived there about noon. Mr. Birch and I were up all night, and in the morning I left for Miscouche, where I remained all day, and performed several operations in that vicinity for Joseph Simmons, Henry Craswell and others. Mr. Craswell drove me to Summer-side on Thursday evening, and on Friday morning I started for home. No sooner had I reached here, than I was insulted and threatened. Then I learned that on Wednesday night, while I was in Alberton, the tramp had entered a house on King Square, and the people said it was me. Now, Sir, for the last six months, I have been slurred and insulted on the streets, in the shops, and even in the churches, and been pointed out as the tramp, so that on the Sabbath, instead of going to church, I remain in my office for peace and quietness. I am no tramp, thief, nor drunkard, and I owe no man one cent. I have my rights as a British subject, and this Island is as free to me, as it is to any man, so long as I conduct myself properly, and I have stood insults until patience has ceased to be a virtue, but I will not be insulted with impunity any longer. My faults are many, and my past life is not blameless, but since I have been here, I have molested or insulted no one, and try to be civil, obliging, and respectful to everybody, and people ought to give me fair play. Whoever is going about at nights will be caught, and then the public will see who the real tramp is. I have something else to do than tramp the streets all night, and I want the police and all decent men to watch my actions, both day and night, for my actions are open for investigation. There are lots of bummers and loafers who do no work, but bum people on the streets for money to get rum with, and no one insults them . . . . Hoping to hear no more insinuations about this tramp business, ...

I remain, respectfully,
J.H. Whitman
(The Daily Examiner, 9 September 1884)

Despite Whitman's protestations, the insinuations did continue. That in the months following there had been a brief interlude in this activity, which coincided with Whitman's absence while he served a term in prison, did little to allay the suspicion that he was indeed the guilty party. His intention to resume business in the city met with strong opposition:

Sir, — . . . The tramp comes here under an assumed name, and acquires a reputation as a skilful veterinary surgeon, and is patronized by those who delight in horses. If I am not misinformed he was caught in the house of R. Bridges, Esq., but let off. He was convicted by a Prince County jury, and sentenced by the Chief Justice to one year's imprisonment in the Prince County Jail, which term has expired, or is about to expire.

Now there are two ways of getting rid of this character, if he reappears in our midst. The first and most effective would be: Let us call in "Judge Lynch," and if he is found guilty, there are tall trees in the Royalty! The other is, "boycott him." Let any citizen who harbors or employs him in any way be boycotted. Let such person be isolated and shunned as we would the small-pox. If this is done, the tramp will soon make tracks for parts unknown.

Your obedient servant,
Old Citizen
(*The Daily Examiner,* 3 October 1885)

It is unclear whether Whitman did, indeed, serve a sentence in the Prince County jail. Others, however, urged a more common measure of dealing with vagrants:

Sir, — . . . Lynching is, of course, out of the question, and Boycotting is impracticable. Simple and effective means can be made use of without breaking the law or wasting time in Boycotting. If a vagrant become a nuisance, the authorities give him so many hours to follow the Kerry Gow's advice and "lave the country." There never was a greater nuisance, nor a more troublesome vagrant, than this man, whether he be guilty or not, and if he be arrested as a nuisance as soon as he comes to town, and ordered to leave the city within a few hours, upon pain of imprisonment, we will quickly be rid of our dangerous visitor, without resortingto protracted or illegal measures.

Yours, etc.

A.H.A.

(The Daily Examiner, 6 October 1885)

What part Whitman played in "the tramp's" activities must remain ambiguous. That they could engender such condemnation suggests the community's fear of disorder, which they believed the vagrant, the beggar, the itinerant underclass might possibly forge if unchecked.

AT MONCTON STATION

Tramps and vagrants congregated around Moncton's railway station, as they did on Charlottetown's streets. Authorities sought to discourage the inevitable loafing around the waiting rooms, but without success. The station and surrounding neighborhood could not escape the colorful and disreputable itinerants who visited many Maritime communities in the late nineteenth century. In October, 1881, Constable O'Rourke arrested one James Flanagan for being drunk in the waiting room. While there he also spotted a teenage girl, Eliza Berry, also under the influence of liquor. She had taken off all her clothes apparently under the mistaken impression that she was in her own room and had retired to her couch. O'Rourke found her asleep with her head resting in the station's coal box and her feet on the stove's pan. The Constable borrowed a coat to cover her nakedness, and took her and her companion to the lock-up. She was well known to the Court as an "old offender"; she was sentenced to three months at Dorchester for vagrancy. Her bizarre behavior continued. Given the run of the corridor before her transfer, the next morning she opened all the doors of the lock-up's cells and allowed the other prisoners, mostly common drunks, to escape.

A tramp named McCarthy was found lying on the street near the railway crossing so drunk that he could not see, hear or move,

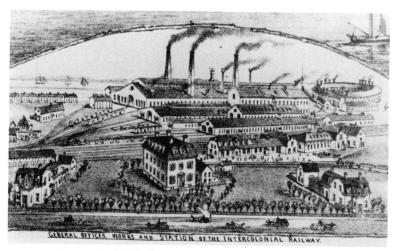

Intercolonial Railway, Moncton. *(Moncton Museum)*

and had to be carried to the police station. He was released after he sobered up and promised to leave Moncton at once. As both Berry and McCarthy illustrated, drink was the common nemesis of many of Moncton's tramps and vagrants. In late May, 1885, Marshal Thibideau discovered an old woman lying drunk under some trees near the station. She had been out in the rain and was in a pitiable condition. She gave her age as sixty-one, and said she had just come out from Scotland, reaching Moncton only the night before.

As in Charlottetown, however, tramps were not only perceived as threats to themselves. Some took advantage of the citizenry. During the winter of 1882, Charles Wortman gave lodging for a few days to a short, stout man who gave his name as Pat Kelly from P.E.I. On the morning of the third day he departed, taking with him Wortman's coat, valued at $6. That householder was also victimized in the same way by another tramp, who made off not only with a coat, but also a pair of pants and two shirts. Monctonians urged the police to curb the flow of such "worthless looking characters."

Killers, Thieves, Tramps & Sinners

He was found on the beach near Sandy Cove with a bag of crackers and a flask of water. His legs had been recently amputated at the knees. An outward bound ship had been seen in the bay the day before. That was the only clue as to how this stranger arrived. None could understand his language. He said his name was Jerome and his ship *Il Columbo*, of which there was no record. He did not seem like a man who had been a seaman or who had done much manual labor. The Overseers of the Poor initially took charge of him. He was taken to Meteghan River, where he was placed under the care of a Corsican, named John Nicholas. Nicknamed "the Russian," it was assumed that he would understand the stranger's dialect. Nicholas had come here after serving as a soldier of the Sardinian contingent in the Crimean War. Nicholas himself was difficult to understand, as he regularly intermixed French and Italian.

Not long after his removal to Meteghan River, Jerome and "the Russian" had a falling-out. The stranger, taking umbrage at being chastised for something he did, refused to talk to anyone again. Almost thirty years later, now an old man, he was under the care of Dedia Comeau, at Cheticamp in Digby County. The nature of his language continued to puzzle local residents. Visitors who understood foreign dialects were regularly brought by to see if they could converse with him. None could. Jerome's identity could only be speculated upon:

> One cannot observe this mysterious character without believing that either his mental faculties are afflicted (possibly through the accident that necessitated the amputation of his feet), or else that he is bound by some terrible oath never to reveal his history or identity. The latter theory, though really not very plausible, appears however to obtain more largely.

> The unfortunate individual was probably once an obstacle in the way of the acquisition, by relatives, of perhaps valuable property, which only his removal could

ensure, hence his being spirited away to spend his re-
maining days a crippled pauper among strangers . . . .

(The Digby Weekly Courier, 7 July 1893)

Jerome remained a mystery until the day he died. He was not
the only such stranger to appear in the County. Centreville, on
Digby Neck, was visited by a tramp named Knowles. Some said he
claimed to be a native of Annapolis, but this was doubted. He arrived in the summer of 1892 and survived by fishing. In the fall
he took shelter in an old loft, earning a livelihood by cutting wood
and doing odd jobs about the town. Equally as mysterious as
Jerome, Knowles when alone was seen thrashing an imaginary
enemy, grasping his own throat, and swearing quite loudly.

Both Jerome and Knowles were not necessarily typical of the
vagrants or tramps who visited Digby and the surrounding area.
Nor was the reception given them as sympathetic. As in Charlottetown, indeed, vagrants were viewed as possible threats to social
order, as part of the "dangerous class." In late 1877 many of these
transients seemed to be on the move, leaving the eastern States and
"overflowing into the dominion." The threat they represented was
sharply underscored:

> Where they find a house unprotected, they are insolent
> robbers, where they meet resolute men, they are impor-
> tunate beggars or sly thieves. To these vagabonds, incen-
> diarism offers a great opportunity of plunder, with little
> or no risk, for as yet we have heard of no salutary punish-
> ment inflicted on those who have been detected. A good
> dry, warm shelter in a jail, with plenty to eat and drink,
> during the inclement season or winter, is no terror to
> them, but the very contrary — especially in places like
> this, where our prisoners are kept in idleness, and sup-
> ported by the taxes obtained from the industrious and
> frugal.

(The Digby Weekly Courier, 9 November 1877)

Whether this threat was real or not — and compared to
Charlottetown, it appeared to be less evident in Digby — vagrants

Digby Harbour. (PANS)

were not welcome. Nonetheless, they were not always arrested, even if they were found to be involved in petty theft or misbehavior. Ratepayers were unwilling to support them in jail. Laws to control vagrants were viewed as a "mere dead letter." The call for more effective punishment was heard:

> The punishment for vagrancy is imprisonment. But as ratepayers seem to prefer to be robbed by the "tramp," rather than pay a tax for his maintenance in jail, why not make said tramp work for his living during his confinement? Our thieves, native and foreign, have a hatred for regular employment. It is support in idleness that makes the shelter of a jail, like ours, desirable. But a cheap shed in the jail-yard, in which prisoners should be compelled to earn their living, by hewing and breaking stone, for building and highway purposes, would have a most salutary effect. Some of the prisoners could be kept at this, some at picking oakum, or some could be sent out,

in a chain-gang to repair the roads, under the care of a keeper. Flogging, also, for petty larceny and kindred offences, would have a very deterrent effect. Our jail would then be a terror — not an attraction — to evildoers, and would be shunned like a pest-house. Shall we try this plan, as our sagacious neighbours in Yarmouth do — or shall we let the runagates wander about at will and invade us in increasing numbers, until our county becomes a Paradise for tramps, and our town falls a prey to the villainous incendiary?

(*The Digby Weekly Courier,* 9 November 1877)

The perceived problem did not disappear. Almost two decades later the "band of wandering vagrants" was seen to be increasing daily and public safety again threatened. As members of an "itinerant underclass," vagrants were classified as a threat to public order; that the real "menace" they represented was much less the case did not diminish such fear.

An especially revealing illustration of the community's response to the vagrant occurred in the waning days of the century. In early December, 1899, an eighteen- or nineteen-year-old youth, named Joseph Hunt — alias Joe Pollock — was arrested and tried under the Speedy Trials Act for setting fire to a small shed off Water Street. Seeking shelter for the night, he had entered the building. On awakening the next morning, he lit his pipe, but was unable to prevent the straw and packing on which he had been sleeping from catching fire. The Court found Hunt innocent and concluded that the fire had occurred by accident. The Magistrate, however, reminded all of the danger to Digby of allowing such homeless men to wander about, sleeping in barns and outhouses. He rebuked authorities for not prosecuting Hunt for vagrancy, for which he was liable to six months' imprisonment with hard labor. The Magistrate suspected this neglect reflected that reluctance to avoid the expense of supporting the vagrant in jail. Indeed, before the prisoner was arraigned, some of Digby's residents sought to convince Hunt to plead guilty. If he had done so, the Judge would have been bound to have sentenced the prisoner to a much longer term at Dorchester, thus relieving the town of any expense for his care. The Magistrate, however, intervened, refusing to accept such a plea unless made so under the advice of counsel. After the appointment of Mr. Munroe to defend Hunt, the prisoner pleaded innocent.

The anomalous response to vagrancy was illustrated by this case. On the one hand, the vagrant, as an outsider to the existing social order, was viewed as a threat which required vigorous control. At the same time, a penurious attitude to public expenditures created some reluctance to enforce the laws against vagrancy or at least to ensure that the sentence would be such that the burden of support did not fall on local ratepayers. This attitude influenced many aspects of Digby's criminal justice system.

THE ILL-TREATED SAILORS

Halifax and Saint John, as port cities, were marked by the presence of numerous sailors on their streets and in their boarding-houses in the nineteenth century. Many of these seafarers were strangers in port. By the 1890s one-third of the sailors in the British merchant marine were foreign-born. On shore, during their stay between voyages, they were relatively isolated and segregated from the wider community. Cast as part of the "disreputable poor," the seamen were often viewed as a nuisance, prone to drunkenness and violence. The local courts which saw many of them from time-to-time showed little sympathy to their plight. The demands of capital took priority over the conditions of labor. "Crimps" or agents who helped find crews for visiting ships found it lucrative to encourage desertion. The illegal actitivies of these brokers represented a serious problem in the Halifax of the 1880s.

The lot of the nineteenth-century seaman was an especially difficult one. Poor working conditions, subjection to onerous contractual obligations, inadequate wages, and inhumane treatment by officers gave little truth to the "romance of the sea." In response to their plight, sailors became frequently embroiled in litigation, work stoppages, and other forms of protest. Yet they found little solace in the majesty of the law, as the *Moss Glen* affair of 1884 illustrated.

The *Moss Glen* was a British barque, registered in Saint John, and arrived in Halifax on the 24th of September, 1884, having sailed from New York. Two days later, the ship's master, Isaiah B. Morris, had six of his men — Henry Alterman, Oscar Kisterman, Charles Doherty, George M. Emptage, Hans Christman and John Jenson — brought before the Stipendiary Magistrate for refusing to

147

Halifax harbour, 1883. (PANS)

do work and obey his lawful orders while aboard the ship. These members of the crew had shipped at New York under articles for two years, which stated they they were to stay with the barque to any ports of the known world, except Greenland. The captain had procured the men through the assistance of boarding house "runners." Apparently Morris had promised the crew an advance on their wages, but this was not recorded within the shipping articles which were required to be certified by the British consul at New York. Realizing that the captain would not abide by the agreement, before the ship left New York the men wished to go ashore and asked the captain's permission to contact the British Consul, refusing to do any work until their request was granted. Morris refused to allow the men ashore. Bound on disciplining them, he left the ship himself and returned with a tug load of men, called "sluggers." These thugs were let loose among the crew, attacking them with belaying pins and shovels. The captain and his first mate watched the melee from the quarter deck, encouraging the assault. When it was over, they invited the "sluggers" into the cabins and offered them liquor and other refreshments, as the beaten crew attended to their wounds. The captain won this battle. As his hired thugs left the ship at Staten Island, the subdued men had no alternative but to do their work as best they could. Their submissiveness did not assuage the ship's master. Throughout the whole trip to Halifax they were overworked and underfed.

When the barque finally arrived at Halifax, the ill-treated sailors demanded to be allowed ashore so that they could lodge a complaint before a magistrate under the provisions of the Merchants Shipping Act. The captain refused. They waited for 24 hours and tried again, also serving notice that they would not work on the ship until their request was acceded to. The confrontation was starting to escalate, as the men wrote to naval authorities advising them of their grievance. Acting on the advice of his agents and attorneys in Halifax, Morris decided to allow one or two ashore, but not those with the most visible bruises suffered from the earlier assault. This did not settle the matter, as the men still refused to work. Rather than resort to bringing in "sluggers" again, the captain sought to discipline his crew through resort to legal measures. He took out a warrant for their arrest and had them brought ashore by the police.

At the trial in police court the counsel for the aggrieved seamen contended that their shipping had been illegal. The American consul was called to verify that no advances were allowed to be paid for the shipment of seamen in the United States. The Magistrate took several days to consider legal objections to the shipping articles under which these members of the *Moss Glen* crew had been taken on. In the end, as had happened frequently in the past, the court ruled in favor of the captain. The Magistrate did feel some leniency was due: "I do not feel disposed, however, to view the offence with severity and if the men return to their duty they will be discharged — otherwise they will be imprisoned in the city prison for two weeks with hard labor." The seamen were quick to respond that they would rather go to prison for six months than return to their ship. Their wish was respected and they were sent to Rockhead, the city prison.

Their ill treatment had not ended. The morning of their fifth day in jail, to their suprise, the seamen were released and hurried off to Richmond where they were put on board a tug and taken to the

Moss Glen. Within an hour afterwards, the ship and recalcitrant crew were on the sea bound for Dunkirk, France.

On receiving his seamen back, the captain was heard to boast that "he would make the b_____s work their way across or starve them to death" (*The Halifax Morning Herald,* 9 October 1884).

The majesty of justice and law had been found neither ashore nor on the sea.

THE "UNNATURAL" ACTS

The strongest condemnation in Maritime communities in the late nineteenth century was reserved for those guilty of "unnatural" acts. These included a variety of sexual offences. In 1889, George P. Niles was charged with having committed adultery with Alice Dale, wife of Andrew R. Dale and his own daughter five years earlier at Botsford, in Westmorland County, New Brunswick. He had also raped his daughter before her marriage. Inexplicably, when Alice was called to testify, she refused to answer any questions lest by doing so she would incriminate herself. The Judge dealt severely with the hapless woman, sending her to Dorchester for contempt of court (New Brunswick Provincial Archives). The conviction against Charles Wright in 1897 for raping a twelve-year-old girl in Fredericton was sustained in the Supreme Court of New Brunswick.

Adultery was included in the list of "unnatural" acts, and could invoke severe punishment, as one John W. Colpitts discovered in 1902. Four years earlier he had married his wife Ella at Moncton. Their domestic life was not peaceful. They quarreled continually, and Colpitts allegedly abused his wife. In May, 1901, Ella decided she could no longer live with him. Leaving him and her two children, who were later placed with the Salvation Army in Saint John, she lived for a time elsewhere in Moncton and then moved to Saint John, where she was able to obtain work. Some time after his wife's departure, Colpitts himself left Moncton and went to Boston. He returned accompanied by a young woman, Bessie Estabrooks. They lived in a common-law arrangement, first in the house of Colpitts' brother, Howard, and then in their own residence in Moncton. There Ella found them, to her chagrin. She immediately laid charges. Colpitts was arrested for "unlawfully cohabiting and living in conjugal union with a woman not his wife, he being a married man." The accused was found guilty, and was sentenced to two years in Dorchester. His punishment included more than confinement to prison. The Judge instructed that he be whipped. On entering Dorchester he was to receive ten lashes with a cat-o'-nine-tails. At the end of the first year and again ten days before his discharge, the whipping was to be repeated.

Nova Scotia, too, was not free of those who engaged in "unnatural" acts, as several cases in 1885 illustrate. Two men in Halifax were charged with the rape of a prostitute, Annie Densore. One of the assailants was successfully convicted. That she was a "fallen woman," the Chief Justice observed, was no excuse for this outrage: "She was a human being and a woman, and entitled to the full protection of the law. Men should aid her to reform and lead a new life, not force her to continue a life of shame and degredation" (*The Halifax Morning Herald*, 24 October 1885). There was less sympathy for a chaplain, a shoemaker, and a fisherman.

THE IMMODEST CHAPLAIN

In late January, 1885, the Rev. W.J. Lough, junior garrison chaplain, was charged by Ann Talbot, wife of a sergeant of the army hospital corps, with using indecent language toward her, indecent exposure of his person, and putting his arms around her. The supposed reputability of the defendant attracted considerable interest in the case within Halifax society.

Mrs. Talbot testified before the Stipendiary Magistrate:

I am married. My husband is William Talbot. He is a sergeant of the medical staff corps. We have been married four years. We were married by Rev. Mr. Simpson. We lived twelve months in Cunard Street and three years in the military hospital. We had three children, two now living. I am not very acquainted with Mr. Lough. He was not in the habit of coming to my quarters before Christmas week. I am a Roman Catholic; my husband is Church of England. About two years ago he [Rev. Lough]

Interior, Wellington Barracks, Halifax, Nova Scotia, c.1905. (PANS)

visited me after the death of my child. On Christmas week he visited me every day. He used merely to ask after the children, myself and husband. I never asked him to call. He never spoke of spiritual things upon these occasions. He visited me only in the day time. We have only one room in which we all live.

My husband was not present any time when Mr. Lough called. Mr. Lough used to be calling upon a sergeant's sick wife and after visiting her he used to come into my room. He called on Jan. 3rd 1885 in the afternoon. My husband was at Dartmouth skating. I had no idea when my husband would be back. He did not say. Mr. Lough knocked at my door on this afternoon, and I said "Come in." He entered and shook hands with me and asked after the children. He said to me, "Mrs. Talbot, you are always in good health and cheerful." I said, "I am always the one way." He asked what I meant by that. I said, " Cheerful, sir." I was rubbing the neck of the child's night dress, and Mr. Lough asked, "What are you doing there, Mrs. Talbot[?]" He said, "Bring it to me." I took a little book in my hand and sat down by the fireplace. He said, "What are you fooling there for, Mrs. Talbot; come over and talk to me." I went over and stood beside the table, and he again asked me for my hand. He said, "You are the one woman I want to get over, Mrs. Talbot," and he repeated my name three times as follows: "Oh! Mrs. Talbot; Oh! Mrs. Talbot; Oh! Mrs. Talbot." Turning around, I said, "What do you mean Mr. Lough by coming to my quarters to insult me while my husband is away and you a minister of God?" I went to the door to go out and he followed me, and put his arms around my neck. I pushed him away from me, and went out of my room and downstairs.

I wouldn't have been able to get out of the room only that the door was a little open at the time. I nearly knocked Mr. Lough down trying to get away from him. He had hold of me by the neck and was trying to kiss me, but I did not give him a chance. The children were asleep. When he had his arms around my neck I smelled liquor on him. When I got out of the room I went down to the wardmaster's office to report the affair to the senior noncommissioned officer. Failing to find him, I told Corpl. Tough who was in the office what had occurred. The office was a flight of stairs below my quarters. I saw a cabman below and he said he was waiting for Mr. Lough. I told him he had better go up in my quarters and tell him to come down. I then went to Corpl. Tough's quarters and told the affair to Mrs. Tough. I remained there till I thought Mr. Lough had gone. I was much excited when I rushed out of my room. I scarcely knew what I was doing.

. . . Mr. Lough officiated as clergyman at the funeral of my child. That is the first time I ever met Mr. Lough. Mr. Lough is not required to call at the hospital every day. About a week before Christmas Mr. and Mrs. Lough called on me, but they didn't stay long . . . . The night of the occurrence I told my husband and he reported the af-

*Changing the guard at Wellington Barracks, Halifax,
c.1890-1900. (PANS)*

fair to Lieut. Towers . . . . Up to the time I took up the
book to read in my room I never suspected anything of
Mr. Lough. I thought he was acting strangely with me,
but as he was a clergyman I imagined it was all right.

I have been married twice. My first husband is dead.
My first child by my present husband is dead. She was
16 months old. I don't know how long it was after we
were married that the child died. I understand my first
husband was killed in Boston. I heard he fell from the
rigging of a ship. I never wrote to find out if my husband
was killed . . . .

The chaplain, as another witness testified, apparently upset
more than one woman that day:

Sergt. Birrell sworn: I am stationed at the military hospital. I saw Mr. Lough at the hospital on the Saturday afternoon in question. He was in my quarters about four
o'clock. When I came in he shook hands with me. He
afterwards made a short prayer. He seemed to be excited
and I concluded he had been drinking. He shook hands

with my wife, and continually repeated, "Don't forget your God." He put his face very near my wife's face, and shook her hand very roughly. I was not in when he first entered my quarters. My wife sent for me. I understood I had been sent for on account of Mr. Lough's strange manner. When he left my quarters he went towards Mrs. Talbot's quarters, but I did not see him enter. There was a nurse present with my wife at the time. It didn't occur to me at first that anything was wrong with Mr. Lough. I don't think he is an excitable man. I never noticed anything about his manner before that I would attribute to drink. His voice on this occasion was strange. He acted like a man under the influence of liquor.

(*The Halifax Morning Herald,* 22 January 1885)

THE REPULSIVE SHOEMAKER

Thomas Reno was a Halifax shoemaker whose workshop was located on Barrington Street, opposite Macdonald's foundry. A widower and grandfather of about sixty, short in stature and of rather stout build, he had been a resident of the city for much of his life. As far as the police were concerned he had heretofore an unblemished record. In October, 1885, the suspicion that he was the perpetrator "of a repulsive and unnatural crime" was confirmed by Halifax police. It was learned that for some months he had been in the habit of enticing young, innocent and unsuspecting little schoolgirls into his shop by treating them with pennies and candies. Once inside the shop he carried out his "beastly revellings." Based on evidence from several sources, the police raided his establishment and found two victims, both under the age of eleven, on the premises — one little girl upstairs and the second in the ground flat close beside Reno. He was immediately arrested and taken to the station. The girls signed affadavits and told in a simple straightforward manner what he had done to them. A medical examination was scheduled to determine if they had been criminally violated. Reno protested his innocence, alleging that the girls had simply come to his shop to play.

The Marshal could recall few parallel cases in Halifax in his memory. One similar incident had occurred a short time before, but had been hushed up (*The Halifax Morning Herald,* 28 October 1885).

THE INCESTUOUS FISHERMAN

The most "unnatural" act of all, incest, regretfully was occasionally discovered in the rural parts of Nova Scotia. Levi Snow, a 45-year-old fisherman, lived at Parker's Cove in Annapolis County. His daughter, Esther, was an attractive looking young woman and was engaged, over her father's objections, to a man named Wier. With the marriage appearing imminent, the father attempted to drown his daughter. She immediately had him arrested on four charges:

1. with assaulting and attempting to murder her;
2. with committing a rape upon her when she was under twenty years of age;
3. with raping her when she was over twelve years of age; and
4. with maintaining incestuous relations with her.

Judge Ritchie, recently appointed to the Supreme Court bench, heard the case. The only witness was Esther herself. She swore that nine years earlier, when she was but a child, her father had taken her in a small boat across the cove where they lived for the ostensible purpose of gathering firewood. While there, under threat of killing her with an axe, he forced himself upon her.

Apparently, this abuse had been subsequently repeated. Snow was found guilty. Ritchie, in passing sentence, observed that "the case was without precedent in the history of Nova Scotia, the extreme penalty for which was death. He had no desire to hurry him into eternity, and to enable him to prepare for that end to which all were hastening, he would send him to the penitentiary for life."

During the brief trial, Snow's wife appeared in court, but showed little concern at either the crime or the sentence (*The Halifax Morning Herald,* 9 October 1885).

THE NEGLECTFUL HUSBANDS

Disorder and challenges to the rule of law periodically marked not just the streets and barrooms of Maritime communities. Though less sensational, discord within the family nonetheless could have an impact equally as significant. This was especially the case for those married women whose husbands wavered in their duty. Elizabeth Parker and Leah Maisner, albeit from very different backgrounds, were similarly aggrieved against neglectful husbands.

In January, 1899, Elizabeth Hannah Parker charged her husband, William B. Parker of Halifax, with failing to support her "whereby her health is likely to become permanently injured." After a violent confrontation, Parker took the children and left his wife bereft of all but a few possessions.

DEPOSITION OF ELIZABETH PARKER

I live in Halifax. I am the wife of the accused. I have been stopping at my father's since last Wednesday week. I was married ten years ago the 9th of last November by Mr. Rogers, Methodist Minister. After our marriage we lived on corner of Blowers and Albermarle Streets. I lived with my husband the accused until last Wednesday week. Last Monday week my husband and I with two others were to go to visit Mrs. Bristow's on Falkland St. He came home that day at 6:30 p.m. The trouble between us took place on Monday night. On Tuesday and Wednesday he took all the furniture in our house away and took away the children. I was in the house at the time he was removing the furniture. I did not forbid him nor ask him to support me. The last time I had a meal with my husband was last Monday week. He has not given me anything towards any support. I collected $7.00 service from Charles Holland, a tenant of my husband's. He did not use to pay me the rent except when my husband was out. I spent $4.00 on myself and children before I left the house. I got the money on Saturday before the trouble, got it on the fourteenth of the month. I left the house last Wednesday week. There was nothing in the house except a stove and a dresser. There was no food in the house. My husband was at the house until the things were cleared out. I have been recently under the care of a physician — Dr. Clusholme — was sick for six weeks just before Christmas. I was getting stronger than I had been in health[?] when the trouble took place. My health has been poor since my husband left me. I am troubled with weakness and palpatation of the heart. I have eaten only what neighbours give me. I got nothing from my husband since he left me. My husband works as a carpenter at the Royal Engineer works. He gets eight shillings a day. I have four children living and two are dead. My husband indulges in drink. He often did not get home till between twelve and two o'clock in the morning. Last Monday night week he took me by the throat and threw me on the bed and nearly choked me. I have always been troubled with heart trouble. I never had good health and have been worse since he left me. My health is worse than before. I have gone cold and hungry through worrying for my children and because I had no money to buy food. I have met my husband twice since on the street. I know that my husband visits daily the liquor shops of Thompson Chalmers and Doyle; late and early he visited them. He would come home drunk.

I received the $7.00 between seven and eight o'clock the Saturday before the trouble. I spent $1.00 on Saturday evening for household necessaries and fifty cents on Sunday. I spent some more on Monday. I bought no liquor on Monday. I had some liquor on Monday. The money my husband found was kept in a drawer of which I had the key. He often left money in the drawer. Sometimes he brought no wages home. He paid bills with it. There was no money in the drawer on Saturday until the $7.00 less $2 was put in — $2.00 of that amount I retained to spend on other things. A fortnight ago last Saturday I was in a neighbor's house — Mrs.

159

Carmichael's. I had $15.00 with me then. Out of that amount I paid $7 to two parties and put balance in the drawer. What my husband left of the balance I took to spend for the house. I tore up no notes at Mrs. Carmichael's on the 6th of January last nor at any other time. I broke no dishes at Mrs. Carmichael's at any time.

My husband came home about six o'clock or after on Monday the 16th January. I was not then under the influence of liquor nor at any other time that day until after the trouble took place. My husband's tea was ready. My sister was there. I don't know whether she had been drinking. We were to have gone to Mr. Bristow's that evening. My husband refused to go. He did not give as a reason for refusing that I was not fit to go. I did not tell my husband to my knowledge that he had accused me of being drunk and that I was then drunk, having drank two flasks of whiskey. Don't remember telling him anything to that effect. I very often drink intoxicating liquor. The dispute between my husband and I took place in the presence of my sister. I don't know whether his brother was present or not. I slept that night in the kitchen on the lounge. There were dishes smashed that night in the kitchen. I smashed all that belonged to me. I smashed a considerable quantity. My husband was at the kitchen door when I did it. I was in a tantrum. My husband has smashed dishes when he was in liquor. He smashed two chairs within a year — about six or seven months ago. I do not know where my children are. I have inquired on Maitland St. but have not been able to find out. He took my children away in my absence. I never asked him as to where they were. I have not asked him for support. I knew where he worked and where I could find him. My husband was paid last Friday or last Friday week. I have not asked him for money. I have seen my husband often in one of the liquor shops. I have sent for him by his brother once or twice. I took away my own personal effects.

I have been stopping with my father since last Wednesday week. He lives on Brunswick Street. I never visited at Mr. Clancey's on corner Grafton and George Streets. I have been under the influence of liquor occasionally. Some of the times my husband and my brother-in-law brought the liquor to me. I was convicted once in Police Court for using abusive language. My husband paid the fine. My husband never took me home in a drunken condition. On one occasion I was at Mrs. Melvin's. He came for me and took me home and beat me. I went back to Mrs. Melvin's. He then brought a policeman there to take me home. I did not go till next morning. I had been drinking porter and wine at Mrs. Melvin's. I was not under the influence of liquor. I do not think I was drunk as I walked from Maitland to Cunard Streets. I was never so drunk that I could not walk, except that Mrs. Melvin may have given me some after I went to bed at her house. I left my house between seven and eight o'clock in the evening last Wednesday week. I went to my father's.

The only things in the house where I left were an ice chest, stove and dresser. No mattresses there. I have since been at my father's. I have not since been back to the house. I have been going out every day. I have been getting my breakfast each morning at my father's. I have had my dinner sometimes at Mrs. Costis', sometimes at Mrs. Reid's, and at other times at Mrs. Bristow's and Mrs. Allen's. I get my tea at my father's and sleep there.

I can't say how many dishes I destroyed last Wednesday week. I destroyed different articles. No dishes belonging to my husband were destroyed by me. I was perfectly sober at the time. I was in a temper at the time. I destroyed them on account of a beating he gave me an hour or two before. I did not often go out of the house in the daytime. I left my children sometimes with Mrs. Carmichael's children when I went with him. I remember the last time my husband was to Hubbard's Cove. I did not leave the house in his absence.

I was convicted in Police Court for abusive language to my step-mother. She is living with my father now. I am welcome at my father's home. He is poor. The incident with regard to Mrs. Melvin occurred I think more than twelve months ago. My husband came and took the furniture away. I authorized Mr. Power as my solicitor to demand support from my husband.

(Halifax Magistrate's Court, RG 42 Series C, Vol. 2, #24
[Parker, 1899], Public Archives of Nova Scotia)

Leah Maisner unsuccessfully sought support from her husband, whom she had married in Warsaw. In her testimony she attempted to convince the Court that her marriage had been valid, that her husband had deserted her in Poland, and that they had not been divorced. Despite her efforts, the case against a neglectful husband was not sustained.

DEPOSITION OF LEAH MAISNER

I live on Gottingen St. I know the prisoner (pointing to defendant). That is him.

I met him in Europe years ago. He was my cousin. My mother and his father were brother and sister.

Defendant is my husband. I was married twenty-three years ago in Warsaw, Russia by the Warsaw Rabbi. My maiden name was Leah Spinnaek.

I was married by the Rabbi and by the police. The Rabbi was "Clapfish." I didn't know the Rabbi previous to the marriage. I didn't get married in a church. I was married at 8 Miller St., Warsaw. I have evidence of that marriage. The paper I have here is my marriage license. I was married at eight p.m. About two hundred people were at the ceremony. Defendant was present, and I was present. He was before the ceremony single. I stood under a canopy with defendant and he swore with the ring I wear that he married me with that ring and that he would love, honour and obey me and that he would love me and be true to death. I swore the same thing in reply. He put the ring on my finger before the Rabbi and the company present. I was then eighteen. Mother and father were present at the ceremony. There were prayers and blessings. The Rabbi acceded to all that went on when the ring was put on. The Rabbi took a page out of a book and Defendant and I signed it, and the Rabbi gave it to me and I kept it. It was part of the ceremony. It is not in Canada. I lost it. I lost this paper about six years after the marriage, possibly seven years after marriage when I moved. I lived eight years after by father and mother's. It always was laying in the drawer. I left it there when I left his house. I left seven or eight years after. Defendant and I lived there seven or eight years. I didn't think of it when I left father's house. It never came into my mind that I should look for it. That paper was called "Exsube." It was a writing. Above the signature was writing to the effect that we agree to marry. . . . I can't read Hebrew language. The Exsube was in the Hebrew language. The Rabbi read and explained the Exsube before I signed it. The Exsube was taken by me to have it translated and certified. The Judge of the Police Court read it to me in the police court. He didn't understand Hebrew. The Rabbi translated it in the Police Court. He was the same Rabbi that married me. The defendant went with me after the marriage ceremony to the Police Court and we both signed our names after a Russian translation of the Exsube was written . . . . I went from the Court to my father's after the wedding ceremony. Defendant and I slept together. I went by the name of Maisner after the marriage which is defendant's real name. We lived together seven or eight years by my parent's house. I had eight children by defendant.

- Defendant first left me ten years after the marriage. He came back and brought with him a baby and took me over to a place called Carlish. He said the baby was sick and he was going for a doctor. That baby was not mine. When he left the first time he took the equivalent of $400 with him.

He left Carlish after two days. He said he was going to the doctor and failed to return. He left and the woman he had as a mistress left about the same time. He left me the baby. I never saw him again till I came to Nova Scotia. He wrote me a letter. I received it about thirteen years ago when I was in Warsaw by my father's in father's house. By my father means at home. It is at home. It is not here now. I answered it, and got another from him. Possibly eight or ten letters received by me. I answered every one. I don't know where they are now. I have not any of them in Canada. It is thirteen years ago since I received them. I don't know where they are now. I used to keep them in a drawer in father's house. They are not there now. He wrote these letters from Boston thirteen years ago, and after he went away the second time he never wrote for twelve years. He never wrote at all after that. I remained there at same address four years to six years. Then I went to a trade and lived with my sister.

About two years ago I came to New York City. I came to Halifax six weeks ago. I went first two days to a Hotel. For the first two weeks I searched for defendant and found his house locked up. I first saw him in another Court. I attended the Synagogue once. I saw defendant there. In his presence and hearing I begged the congregation there to make him support me. It was two weeks ago Sunday possibly. He was about 127... [?] away. I spoke out loud and all of them heard me say I was sick and poor. Geller was present, jumped at my breast and some young people interceded or interfered. After that I sat down awhile and went out. He didn't follow me out. This was after I saw him in the other Court. When in the Synagogue defendant didn't look at me.

I have got no support from him. I am poor, sleeping on chairs and feeling very sick this last six weeks. Every day I am feeling worse. I have weak turns, bad turns from weakness. Every four weeks I have painful menstruations. I have no means to live on. I am in debt for three weeks board and room. I live with a Mr. Ball. I have paid him nothing. They don't want to keep me after today. I fainted several times at Bernstein's and he had the doctor to me twice. I sleep on three chairs. I have no relations here.

I came to America near two years ago a little after Easter. It is pretty near two years I am here. It was at Castle Gardens Island [Manhattan]. I gave the name of Mrs. Snider. (At Hamburg I was asked by the authorities where I was going. I said to look for my husband. They refused to pass me, and I was advised to go under somebody else's name so I went with a Mr. Snider under the name of Mrs. Snider and got a passport to that effect.) I got the passport in Hamburg. I mean I went from there under Mr. Snider's passport under the name of Mrs. Snider. Mr. Snider got his passport in Warsaw.

Mr. Snider altered the passport at Hamburg. The police gave passport at Warsaw. Mr. Snider showed this passport at Hamburg and the authorities there gave him it back and advised me to go under his name to New York as his passport to get through the

Castle Gardens authorities and we had two separate passage tickets under those names.

Mr. Snider travelled in the same train with me to Hamburg. His name is "Ignace Schneider." On the frontier between Poland and Germany I gave no name. I had no passport from Warsaw. I don't know why Snider had a passport and I had none. Snider still lives in New York at 171 Essex St. care of Mrs. Wechler. I lived in New York in the same house.

I knew Snider five to six years before I left Warsaw. He is not a married man. He lived in Warsaw by his sister's. I didn't live in the same house. I lived with my sisters about ten streets away.

Since I came to New York I lived for the first eight days with Mrs. Blaustein a glove cutter and then moved to the first floor of Mrs. Wechler as there was no room for me at Mrs. Blaustein's. From my family I had $32 change and I didn't go to work, but went to the police. For six months I worked at artificial flowers and afterward by gloves. Mr. Schneider [Snider] is a glove cutter from Warsaw. I never introduced Mr. Schneider as my husband to anyone. When asked suggestively as to this, I always denied it. I known Mr. Harry Glube [whose wife was Mrs. Maisner's first cousin] of Halifax. I saw him in New York about five or six weeks ago.

I had no rooms but I slept with a girl boarder there. Mrs. Wechler keeps a boarding house. I never told Glube that Schneider gave me his wages. He never gave me any part of his wages. I borrowed from him at certain times a dollar or two. Out of fun I told Geller that Schneider gave me his wages after being annoyed by Geller or intimidated by him. Geller threatened to have me arrested if I refused to go home next day and said if I would go he would give me $10.

I had been in Geller's house eight days before this threat. I was threatened thus the first morning after the first day I was by Geller's. I was there eight days altogether. When I told Geller Schneider gave me his wages Geller made no reply. I said it to Geller out of fun. He annoyed me every day and I said it out of fun. When I wanted clothes I asked Schneider to assist me with the loan of a few dollars and when I earned it I returned it to him. I never told Miss Geller that Schneider gave me clothes during the stay at his Geller's house. Mrs. Harry Glube is my first cousin. I saw her in Warsaw before she left once on the street.

I didn't know Schneider then. I didn't then meet Mrs. Glube when I was in company with Schneider. I met her when I was in company with a man, father of two children. I don't remember the man's name. Now I recollect his name was "Naddelmen." He was in his father's store.

I didn't tell Glube in New York that I was too cute to have children by Schneider. (The witness is asked what she is laughing at and she said at the children part as ridiculous.) I never said that if I met defendant he could never know I was married or anything like that to Glube, but I was always looking for my husband is what I said to him. When people commenced to insinuate here that I was the wife of Schneider I wrote to him asking him to send an affadavit to contradict it and W.J. Ball got a letter from Schneider addressed to him for me. The letter is in Court.

From the first minute I made up my mind to search for my husband. I didn't hear a year before I left that defendant built a large house in America. Defendant has relatives in Warsaw. I met them frequently but never spoke to them.

I never told Geller that if I got money from defendant that Schneider and I would come to Halifax to live.

I can't write Hebrew but I can write Polish, German and Russian. Defendant cannot write.

Passage money from New York to here cost about $50 in a round about way. Glube in New York gave me $50. I disbursed part and borrowed about $30 to carry on with. I borrowed it from the housekeeper Mrs. Mechler there, with whom I left some things. I paid $3.00 per week board and lodgings in New York. Marriage of cousins is not forbidden in Russian. The "Rabbi" was an authorized rabbi not any relation to either defendant or me. Schneider has the passport.

Defendant didn't divorce me according to Jewish custom. I heard the defendant had sent a divorce to the Rabbi at Warsaw. I sent my sister-in-law to the Rabbi for information as to where defendant was and I heard he was in Boston. This was possibly ten or twelve years ago. I don't know if my sister-in-law took the divorce for me.

I didn't tell Friedman Rabbi here that Maisner divorced me according to Jewish custom and that I sent my sister-in-law for the divorce. I had no conversation with Friedman about a divorce.

I didn't tell Miss Geller that defendant divorced me and that I sent my sister-in-law for the divorce. I had no conversation with Miss Geller as to Meisner divorcing me.

I didn't agree with Glube in New York to get a divorce from defendant for $500 according to the American law. The $50 given me by Glube was given to me out of charity. I know Auerbach and Franklyn, both notaries public. I was two or three times in Auerbach's office. I tried to get the $500 that Goldberg alias Glube offered me to have means to go to Chicago to see defendant. I had an impression that the defendant was there. I didn't demand $3000 or any terms at all but wanted Glube alias Goldberg to tell me where defendant then was. Glube was four times to my lodgings in New York. Glube came to Schneider's . . . [?] and I came up as Glube had appointed six o'clock p.m. Glube met Schneider and me with a man and woman, neighbours in the park in New York one evening. The man's name is Strights and he lives now in Chicago.

I did not consult Auerbach as to whether I could marry Schneider before getting a divorce from defendant. I am not married to Snider.

When I came to New York from Hamburg I slept on one deck with females and Schneider on another deck with the males. I never had sexual relations with Schneider. In New York we slept on different floors. I slept downstairs where female boarders were and Schneider slept upstairs. I didn't write to Schneider but I wrote to Mrs. Wechler to see Schneider and I got a letter from Mrs. Wechler in reply . . . . I never received any divorce. I was always searching for defendant . . . .

[Corrections made by witness.] Defendant's mother and my father are brother and sister. He took away when he left the equivalent of $4000 (not equivalent of $400). I didn't get passport by name of Schneider but passage ticket (Shifscart by that name). I now say I did not go under Schneider's passport but on my own passport and in name on "Shifscart" of Mrs. Schneider. Schneider didn't alter passport at Hamburg. I couldn't get a passport from Warsaw without my husband's signature. I didn't live in Geller's house eight days before the threat. Glube was not four times at my lodgings but at Schneider's. Stright is not in Chicago but in Gloversville near New York.

6 November 1901 — Attorney-General: The King is unwilling to further prosecute this suit against defendant and consents that he shall go thereof without ...

(*Halifax Magistrate's Court,* RG 42 Series C, Vol. 3, #83
[Maisner, 1901], Public Archives of Nova Scotia)

THIEVES, ROBBERS AND CON-MEN

Although only a small community, Charlottetown routinely experienced the petty thefts that occurred in all Maritime cities and towns of the period. Thefts of foodstuffs, household articles, store goods, money, fruit and garden produce, clothing, jewelry, and domesticated animals, were not uncommon. Theft was a crime against property, but more importantly it was a "crime of opportunity"; thieves found ample occasions on the streets, in and around stores, and in residences to steal items that they found desirable:

> On Saturday evening about half-past seven o'clock, a daring attempt was made to rob the store of Messrs E.&B. Smith of a case of boots. The robber entered the front door of the store, and seized a case containing three or four dozen pairs of boots, and made off across Queen Street. A girl who was in the shop at the time, quickly followed him, shouting lustily for the police. There was a large number of people on the Street at the time, and the thief, in order to make his escape, dropped the box, and disappeared in the darkness of Richmond Street. No trace of him has yet been found.
>
> (*The Daily Examiner,* 25 November 1878)

A young fellow named Story perpetrated a most daring robbery at the St. Lawrence Hotel a few days ago. He walked off the street into a room on the third flat, stole therefrom a valuable pipe belonging to one of the boarders, and escaped without apprehension. He will be dealt with as the law directs in a short time.

(*The Daily Examiner,* 3 December 1878)

A few evenings ago a young man who was staying at Mr. Sinclair's boarding house, corner Pownal and Sydney streets, hung his coat, hat and scarf in the main hall of that house previous to taking supper. Shortly after 7 o'clock he heard a noise in the hall; and, thinking it was an unsafe place to hang clothing, he repaired thither to remove his apparel. He was convinced of the unsafety upon arrival, and has since been unable to discover the whereabouts of his coat. The noise heard in the hall, he supposes, was caused by a person entering from the street who ran off with the coat.

(*The Daily Examiner,* 30 January 1879)

Opportunities presented themselves within the domestic unit. Although relatively rare, theft from other members of the family was not unknown:

On Wednesday evening last a man named George Swan was arrested by Officer McGregor, for stealing a purse containing $30 from his mother. He appeared before the Magistrate this morning for examination. The evidence taken shows that at noon on Wednesday he entered his mother's dwelling house and stole the purse from her bedroom. She missed the purse shortly after it was taken, immediately suspected the prisoner of taking it, and left orders at the Police Station for his arrest. He was about "striking out" to have a jolly time. When arrested by the officers in a bar room he was tendering a ten dollar bill for a treat. They immediately searched him and found on his person twenty dollars. The bartender returned to the police the change of the ten dollar bill which was tendered for the drink, and thus Mr. S. only succeeded in squandering twenty cents of the stolen money. He was

committed for trial at the June sitting of the Supreme
Court for larceny.

(The Daily Examiner, 7 June 1878)

Servants, because of the ready access they had to household
goods and articles, were at times not reluctant to take advantage of
their position:

A dishonest servant girl stole a valuable ring from her
mistress (whose residence is on Grafton Street) yesterday, and departed for her home at Wood Islands. The
mistress issued a warrant and proceeded to the paternal
residence of that servant, in the company of a tall
policeman.

(The Daily Examiner, 7 November 1878)

Such thefts, seen as violations of the trust supposedly at the
core of the domestic unit, were condemned. So too were those who
desecrated sacred ground. Occasionally cemetery robbers were at
work in Charlottetown, eliciting a strong response from the "respectable":

Sherwood Cemetery. There are in our midst a number of
unfeeling wretches who do not hesitate to rob the graves
in this "God's Acre." Bereft of all feeling, and deadened
to any impulse of humanity, must be those contemptible
creatures who could thus ruthlessly plunder the last resting place of the dead. We blush to think that even
"ladies" (?) can lend themselves to such a desecration. It
is, however, consoling to know that the officers of the
law are on the track of the thieves who will, we trust, be
apprehended and made realize the enormity of their offence.

(The Daily Examiner, 24 July 1880)

Also drawing occasional condemnation were the activities of
gangs or groups of youths, who committed a variety of petty thefts
in Charlottetown. Storekeepers as well as residents were alert to
their misbehaviour:

Robbery. On Friday evening last a pair of pants were

stolen from the Glasgow House by three young thieves who are as yet unknown. The pants were hanging on a rack in front of the store, and about half-past five o'clock four boys passed the street. Two of these lifted a third one up to the rack, and he seized the pants, and after doing so ran off. A woman named Mugford, who was near the store at the time, recognized one as John Hughes a boy of about 16 yrs. of age. He was arrested. He denies being there or knowing anything about the robbery. He will be further examined on Tuesday.

(*The Daily Examiner,* 22 December 1879)

Hughes was fortunate. The evidence was not sufficient to convict him, and he was discharged. His alleged misadventure was not unique to his age group.

Two young thieves named Alfred Farmer and John Doyle (Corngoose) were arraigned before the Stipendiary Magistrate charged with being two of a gang who of late have been robbing cellars in this city. They are also charged with robbing the till in Mr. Fletcher's Music store some weeks ago. Both were remanded to jail.

(*The Daily Examiner,* 7 December 1882)

Unlike Hughes, these two youthful larcenists were found guilty and sentenced to six months imprisonment with hard labour. This sentence was said to be "richly deserved" as they had been involved in a number of other thefts in the city.

As in other Maritime communities such acts of property crime were frequently those of male youths. Juvenile pickpockets were active during market days, exploiting especially those in from the country. Orchard owners complained of the loss of fruit. Storekeepers both inside and outside their shops found their goods too tempting to crafty lads. The Magistrate sought to deal decisively with these cases. Youths and others charged with larceny were commonly sentenced to jail "with hard labour." Repeat offenders particularly drew the ire of the Court. A young boy in August, 1891, was given three months with hard labour for stealing fruit from the garden of one Mrs. DesBrisay. The sentence was imposed partly because he was described as an "old offender."

Not all cases of theft brought before the Stipendiary Magistrate resulted in conviction. Too hasty an arrest without substantiating evidence led to acquittal:

> Annie Whelan, who was charged with the larceny of a
> quantity of ladies' underclothing from Mrs. Leddell (who
> is now absent from the Province) was today acquitted by
> the Stipendiary Magistrate. The Magistrate said that as
> the things she was accused of stealing were all small, he
> had no doubt that they were given to her by Mrs. Liddell.
>
> (*The Daily Examiner*, 29 September 1879)

In some few cases the accused was able to gain acquittal by furnishing supporting witnesses or by having the charges dropped through promising to return the missing item. At times the charges were redefined in Court, especially if the accused was known to the police:

> *Police Court.* This morning, James Manderson was arraigned charged with the larceny of a dressing case,
> lounge, pair of blankets, two feather pillows and a quilt,
> the property of Mr. Albert R. Crosby, of this city. The articles in question, it was brought out in evidence, were
> stored in Mr. Geo. W. Gardiner's warehouse on Grafton
> Street, from which place they were stolen and sold to a
> man named Savidant, who lives in Gaytown, in whose
> possession they were found by the police. Mr. Crosby
> identified the articles as his property, and Mr. Savidant
> related the facts connected with the purchase of the articles from Manderson, who said he got them from "a
> decent, honourable man," but declined to give his name.
> Manderson, in reply to questions asked by His Honour,
> said he bought the goods from Jos. O'Reilly, a young lad
> formerly in the employ of Mr. Gardiner, and thought that
> the transaction was all right. He said further, that he did
> not give Savidant O'Reilly's name, as in trading it is not

his custom to give names. Marshal Cameron said that O'Reilly did not bear a very good character, and he had seen him and Manderson together on several occasions. His Honour said the evidence was not sufficient to convict Manderson of the actual larceny of the goods, but he would send him down to jail for three months with hard labour, for receiving stolen property, knowing it to be stolen . . . .

(*The Daily Examiner,* 13 January 1891)

The accused, despite the evidence brought before the Court, at the same time were not above taking a more aggressive stance in their own defence, as did one James Murphy:

. . . James Faraday and Thomas Enman were charged with a number of thieveries. It would be rather laborious, thought the magistrate, to examine their numerous offences, and he, making a bulk of the whole, sentenced each prisoner to six months imprisonment with hard labour. James Murphy arrested for larcenies similar to those of Enman, was sentenced to three months imprisonment, with hard labour, for vagrancy. James protested that he was innocent of all charges preferred against him. He said "he was never free from suspicion; and was always arrested for offences of which he was innocent. He might as well throw himself over the wharf, because he could not live in Charlottetown without being looked upon, by the police, with suspicion . . . ."

(*The Daily Examiner,* 21 October 1879)

Defendants sought to minimize their guilt. The argument that they were drunk at the time, however, did not find a sympathetic reception from the Magistrate. That theft could be the act of an individual experiencing significant economic deprivation was not always evident to the community. The link between larceny and poverty was made especially manifest to Councillor Blake in July, 1881, when he received an anonymous letter from a man explaining why he had stolen articles during the past year from the Market House:

" . . . I have been a poor man and in want [of] provisions having been in the market I asked a man for a hundred of flour and he would not trust me with it I saw a bag as you go up the stairs a fours and I tuck it home with me at another time I tuck one quarter of mutton and another time another quarter of mutton and too pigs heads and ½ of hundred of oatmeal 25 lbs of oatmeal and bag I been in another evening in the market pretty late I saw a tub of butter on the stan I saw no one watch me and I tuck a bag of the flour and put in the tub of butter to it I give it to my wife to convay it to the first place she could hide it and she put it in the east end porch of the market seller and was discovered by lewis and the enecent taken for it their is fifty cents to publish this and all persons having lost those articles the money I am going to send Mr. blake which I will trust to act faithful and prove a friend the [c]ity marshall has got another."

The City Marshall received a letter from the same party asking him to assist Mr. Blake in compensating those who have suffered loss by robbing in the market. The writer, after stating that an innocent party suffered for one of the robberies, hoped that the Marshal and family would never want bread, or have to steal it as he (the writer) did.

(The Daily Examiner, 26 July 1881)

That the destitute might steal to survive did not diminish the community's moral assessments of theft and of the thief. The Magistrate, in exercising his discretion by sentencing the guilty to jail with hard labour, both reflected and reinforced those judgments. Crimes against property were perceived as threats to social order as defined by the "respectable."

The moral and legal condemnation of acts of larceny did not inhibit thieves from seeking innovative means in which they might exploit Charlottetown's citizens. Simon White's "gambit" was one noteworthy example:

The Stipendiary Magistrate's Court was thronged this

forenoon. The star of the occasion was Simon White, a familiar character. Since White's coming amongst us, he has followed the occupation of peddlar, and his voice and satchels were familiar to most of our citizens. He would sell articles much cheaper than they could be purchased for in the stores — a feat which the people could not understand — and many had their doubts as to the honesty of the representative of the house of White, dealer in odds and ends. The merchants were informed of these tremendous bargains, but they could not fathom the mystery any more than could the general public. They, however, suspected that White was somewhat light-fingered and determined to watch him. The dry goods store of Messrs. Perkins & Sterns, on Queen St. was frequently visited by White, and many articles were missed from the shelves. Suspicion pointed to White and he was ordered to be "shadowed." On Saturday morning about half-past seven he dropped into the store. The hour being early but two of the clerks were present, one of whom was engaged upstairs. Shortly after White's arrival the clerk downstairs had occasion to go out of the store, leaving him alone. No sooner had he gone than the peddlar took up a roll of linen and put it under his coat for safekeeping. On the clerk's return he asked to be shown some buttons, and the clerk on going to serve him noticed the end of the parcel projecting from under his coat. He took the linen from White who commenced to cry, and ask that he be let off for God's sake, and he would come around and settle matters with the proprietor. On the arrival of the proprietor he accused White of being a thief and said that he had stolen several articles from the store. White admitted that he was guilty and paid for the articles which he had been accused of stealing. He was then released but on the Marshall hearing of the affair White was arrested. When asked what he had to say for himself, White said that the affair was a joke on his part. The

Magistrate did not take the same view of the matter and after volunteering the information that the prisoner was a first-class felon, sentenced him to six months imprisonment with hard labour.

(*The Daily Examiner,* 9 August 1886)

Innovation in thievery at times revealed a certain degree of brazenness, especially when the stolen goods were brought back to the rightful owner in an effort to make a further gain:

The police yesterday afternoon searched the dwelling of an Upper Prince Street woman, suspected of being the party guilty of shoplifting in Sprague's Bookstore a few days ago and found therein a pair of beaded slippers, which Mr. Sprague says were stolen from the store. The facts connected with the shoplifting appear to be as follows: A few days ago a woman and a young girl visited Sprague's store and asked to be shown some boots. The boots were shown and, while the clerk's back was turned, a pair disappeared. Next day when Mr. Sprague was alone in the store, the girl entered and told him that her mother had bought a pair of boots there yesterday, which she would like exchanged for slippers. Mr. Sprague made the exchange and paid the difference in the price to the girl. The girl then left the store. Shortly after her departure Mr. Sprague missed another pair of slippers. The police were at once notified of the circumstance, and the house searched with the results above stated. They are now looking after the shoplifter.

(*The Daily Examiner,* 28 January 1887)

Shopkeepers were mindful of the variety of tactics shoplifters could use first to escape detection but also subsequently to evade prosecution.

Those charged with theft were most frequently of the "underclass" in Charlottetown. However, occasionally the more respectable members of the community were brought before the Court. Inevitably, wider interest than usual focused on their alleged violation of the law. Such occurred in October, 1882, when Henry

Blatch, Chief Clerk of the County Court of Queen's County was tried for the theft of money and notes from the safe in Carvell Bros. counting room. The accused was a former employee of the Carvell firm. Suspicion was directed toward him because it was believed he had been in possession of one of the stolen bank notes. Blatch was widely known in the business community and was recognized as a member of one of Charlottetown's "better" families. Although he was subsequently acquitted, that someone so prominent could be accused of this crime initially shocked the community.

Charlottetown too did not escape the less frequent, but equally inventive, schemes of the "confidence man." In mid-July, 1886, the Bishop of Charlottetown disavowed any association with a man named Deady who represented himself to be a monk and who was collecting money from Catholics for some institution in Ireland. That same month Chief of Police Flynn received a letter from the Chief of the Eureka Detective Agency in Charleston, Virginia, warning him to be on the lookout for a confidence man, named J. Oakley Crawford: "He is an easy, fluent talker and claims to be an intimate acquaintance of politicians and public men. Oakley is a pleasant, gentlemanly fellow in every way, and one who can easily make friends with both sexes" (*The Daily Examiner,* 23 July 1886). His "scam" was the selling of allegedly large tracts of land in West Virginia. A different approach was attempted by two women in September, 1890. They posed as widows seeking assistance to leave the Island. To add credibility to their claims, apparently both had "withered hands" (*The Daily Examiner,* 27 September 1890). Whether they were actually successful in eliciting any sympathy from the populace is unclear.

The citizens of Charlottetown were occasionally duped by itinerant groups and merchants, seeking a quick profit in misrepresenting what they offered the public. In late September, 1882, a group calling themselves I.W. Baird's Mammoth Minstrels advertised that part of the entertainment included a concert by the famed Royal Hand Bell Ringers of London, England. The latter's

Upper Prince Street, Charlottetown, P.E.I., 1894. (PAPEI)

Boston agent quickly issued a public warning that this claim was fraudulent; the "Bell Ringers" had no such plans, nor were they in any way associated with the "Minstrels." The agent, however, assured all that he would endeavour to attempt to book "the real thing" in Charlottetown early in the next season. Local businessmen were especially sensitive to the claims of itinerant salesmen and to the need to protect their own markets against unfair outside competition. That indeed there were unscrupulous salesmen, merchants, and others making the rounds is evident. Those especially likely to be exploited were the "country folk." Charlottetowners were not alone in being the object of a variety of "scams." Peddlers travelled the country roads selling inferior goods at inflated prices. The unwary could be easily conned by a salesman's claim to represent a reputable Charlottetown firm:

> We learn that a person giving the name of Wm. Taylor, a travelling watchmaker, is sailing around the country under false pretences. This "party" represents that he is a relation of the well-known watchmaker, Mr. E.W. Taylor, of this city, and that he is connected with his business. We are requested to state that these representations are

false in every particular; and that as many complaints
have reached Mr. E.W. Taylor from parties who have
been exploited by the itinerant jobber, it would be well
for the public to be on their guard against possible imposition or fraud.

(The Daily Examiner, 6 May 1886)

Country residents were particularly vulnerable when they themselves made their weekly or monthly shopping trek to
Charlottetown. Their alleged lack of sophistication made them easy
targets. The admonition to beware of "swindlers and cheats"
derived as much from the desire to protect the markets of local
businessmen as from any concern for the well-being of country
cousins.

One persistent problem — evident not just in Charlottetown but
elsewhere in the region at the time — was the circulation of counterfeit bills. Detection was difficult in view of the great variety of
legitimate bills that were then issued. Indeed it was observed "a
collection of all the various kinds of bank notes legally issued in
Canada would form quite an interesting museum. It is impossible
for the people to be familiar with the appearance of all these notes"
(The Daily Examiner, 16 July 1886). Not infrequently only a bank
teller was able to detect a bogus bill:

A counterfeit two dollar note on the Union Bank was discovered among a number of notes handed by a gentleman
to the Teller of the Union Bank a few days ago. It appears
to have been in circulation for at least twelve months, and
perhaps would have circulated twelve months longer had
it not fallen into the Teller's hands.

(The Daily Examiner, 21 April 1880)

It was undoubtedly difficult for authorities to trace the origin of
such a note, after it had passed through a number of hands. The
community's business and service establishments were especially
vulnerable to the passing of bogus bills and coins and to the accusation that they were knowing participants in this type of fraud.

Halifax, too, knew the work of thieves, robbers and con-men. Two notorious examples were Jimmy Legg and Mollie Donnelly, both convicted in 1884 for their skilful but illegal crafts.

One Sunday evening the premises of Mary Ann Godwin were broken into and a gold watch and $10 in cash were stolen. Before leaving, the burglars started a fire among some rags. A passerby noticed the flames and helped extinguish the fire. This combination of burglary and arson had been repeated several times before. The North End especially had seen many mysterious incendiary fires, resulting in heavy losses for both property owners and insurance companies. The case was assigned to Detective Nicholas Power, who after investigating several clues quickly arrested the two brothers James and Samuel Legg, who resided in the same house with Miss Godwin.

Power had joined the Halifax Police Force in 1864, and had been promoted to Detective only two years earlier before his encounter with Legg. He had an illustrious and colourful career with the Force, rising to become Chief of Police in 1906. After the arrest of Jimmy Legg and his brother, Power gave a detailed account of the activities of this hoodlum and what he confessed.

A report was made to the marshal that the premises of Miss Godwin, on Gottingen street, had been burglarized and robbed of a watch and chain, and a sum of money on a Sunday night, and then set on fire. I was detailed to investigate the case. I thought there was a chance to discover the perpetrators. I soon came to the conclusion that the burglars and incendiaries must have been people thoroughly acquainted with the house. I learned that James and Samuel Legg lived with their parents in the upper part of the house; and from my previous knowledge of James Legg, I made up my mind that he was the, or one of the, guilty parties. Miss Godwin usually left the key of her side door under the mat in the hall where the Legg boys would likely know it to be. James Legg, when

Nicholas Power, 1917. *(PANS)*

interviewed by me, endeavored to show that the party
who robbed and fired the premises had entered the house
through the back window, and passed out through the
shop door after committing the crime. After a careful examination of the porch that the guilty party would have
had to pass had he entered that way, I failed to find any
marks which would be there if such had been the case. I
was then more than ever convinced of Legg's guilt, and
at once decided to arrest him on suspicion.

I pointed out certain facts to him, the circumstantial evidence against him. He broke down and confessed the whole thing, and implicated his brother Samuel, who was also arrested. James told me where I would find the watch and chain; and confessed that his brother and himself had conspired to rob his place to raise funds, and fired it to cover up the robbery and thus throw the suspicion to others, by opening the shop door and back window. I recovered the watch and chain, where he said it was. Samuel went with me and showed me where it was hid in the cellar. It was arranged between them that Jim was to take the money and Sam the watch and chain. They pleaded guilty before the magistrate and were committed to the supreme court for burglary and arson.

[Jimmy's involvement in other incendiary fires became evident.] It came to our knowledge that James Legg was in the employ of a man named Kent, who keeps a grocery on Brunswick street. During Kent's absence from the city sometime in the spring, a very mysterious fire occurred in his store, and shortly after James Legg closed up the establishment in the evening. This Legg had also been employed with Mr. Hubley, who keeps a feed and grocery store on Windsor street and a very mysterious fire took place there, while Hubley was absent and no one was about the premises, but this James Legg. That looked very suspicious — and more so because there had been quite a number of mysterious fires in the north end within the past two years. I determined to see if Legg had anything to do with these fires in stores in which he was employed, or any of the others, and traced to any reliable source.

Of course, I was aware that any evidence obtained under the circumstances that this was obtained, could not be used against a prisoner. But the people were beginning to be thoroughly alarmed about the number of incendiary fires, and suspicion naturally attached to innocent people.

But these innocent people were under a terrible disadvantage because it is a very difficult thing for a man to prove that he didn't do a thing. Hence, they continued to be under a cloud of suspicion. Another thing was — the evil was growing, and nobody could tell where it would end. The insurance men also were getting exasperated, and besides the losses entailed on individual owners of property, there was a strong probability of another general rise in insurance rates, because of the greatly increased risks from fire bugs. So I determined to make a big effort to discover who the real fire bug was.

James Legg was confined in a large double cell in jail, and felt lonesome. Another man, who was confined in the jail for a slight offence, was put in the same cell. The two men became intimate. And during their companionship Legg frequently boasted of the excitement he had raised in Halifax by firing buildings and committing robberies, stealing horses, etc. He gloried in it, and further boasted that if he should get free of the charge under which he was then confined, he would make it hot for some people in Halifax. Among other things he told his chum that he had set fire to the new building of Gabriel Edmunds, an ex-policeman, on Compton Avenue, and suspicion for which rested on other parties. This was a particularly hard case on Boutlier, the contractor, who had not handed over the house, and consequently had to bear the whole loss, some $500 or $600 — a crushing blow to a poor man. An official investigation was held, but nothing resulted. James Legg was not thought of in that connection. He also boasted of having placed a dozen cartridges the same night behind the shutters of the house occupied by Miss Kent, as a grocery, on Windsor street. [His object was] To have lots of fun at the same time, and afford a diversity of excitement for the citizens. Some of the cartridges exploded, and damaged the sash. The others were discovered next day. This was never reported in the papers. Next he boasted of firing the barn of John Punch on Robie street, in which a valuable horse, wagon, etc., were burned. Loss about $1,500. No insurance. Punch is a poor man. This is Legg's own confession mind you. It is no insane or drunken man's story, but the bravado of a young Halifax rough. Now, let me recount an incident. Mrs. Punch remembers that on the night of the fire, the first party she saw near the barn was James Legg. He sympathized with her, inquired if she knew how it originated, and asked which horse was in the barn; the red or black one? Mrs. Punch didn't know Legg by name then, but now remembers him quite well. His next exploit, as he himself confessed, was to fire a barn owned by Judge Thompson on Windsor street for which an innocent young man named Malder was arrested on suspicion, but discharged for want of proof. Next he tells of a high old time he had one night, in which he made three different fires . . . . Saturday night there were four fires between 10 p.m. and 3 a.m. The first was Judge Thompson's barn, of which I have just mentioned. The next was George Wiswell's barn, or carpenter shop, on Agrico street. His third exploit that night was to fire a shed in the yard of a house on Cornwallis street, occupied by Deputy Sheriff McAlpine. He gloried in originating all these fires, and gloats over how he kept the police and firemen busy that night. The fourth fire was in McNell's saloon, in the Oxford block. But Legg is not suspected of having any connection with that. Just previous to these, he says he fired McPhillips' barn in the north end of Agricola street. Neighbors say they saw a boy of Legg's description running from the barn after the fire was discovered and jumping over a fence.

[Legg also confessed to theft.] He confided to his chum confidentially that two years ago he stole a horse and sleigh belonging to F.C. Stevens, the coal dealer. After enjoying a good drive his conscience smote him, and he returned the horse and sleigh, but retained the handsome buffalo, as a keepsake, and as a memento of his conscientiousness in returning the horse and sleigh. He used the robe as a bed covering during the winter, and sold it in the spring for $5. Now, in proof that Legg told the truth, I may mention that Stevens reported to me that his horse and sleigh had been taken away from the door and returned by a young man, minus the buffalo robe, who said he had found the team straying, and knowing that it was Stevens', returned it. The story was a most plausible one, and Stevens believed it — very thankful to get back his sleigh. I afterward interviewed the man who purchased the robe from Legg, and thus proved that part of the story. That man is now willing to return the robe to Stevens. Legg also confessed to stealing scores of little things, too numerous to mention in detail. He boasts that he has a lot of this stolen property stowed away now in a place where the police can never reach it.

Sam [Legg] appears to have been a sleeping partner in these things. But in connection with the Godwin robbery Jim says they visited Mrs. Godwin's apartments on the previous Sunday, but the amount of cash in the purse being a small quantity, they decided to wait until it had increased. The next Sunday the amount was $12 and they determined to act then, and did so.

He [Jimmy Legg] suggested to his chum many original schemes for breaking out of jail, and novel plans of action after they got out. He was going to get one of his "pals" who visited him, to bring an instrument with which he would loosen some bricks and thus enable him to get into the corridor. This "pal" was also to bring him a revolver which he (Legg) had at home. With this he would shoot Jailer Chambers, take the keys, and thus escape. This was to be done in the dead of night, and after attaining liberty, they promised to make Halifax howl by firing the following places: Demster's kiln, off

West street. Tyler's brush factory, Robie Street, Gordon & Keith's factory, Dundonald St. In the general alarm and excitement as a consequence of these fires, occupying the whole attention of the police and citizens, they would start for the country. Of course, his chum enthusiastically assented to these blood-curdling propositions.

[I believe his stories.] The fires named by him actually took place, at or about the time that he states. Official investigations have been held into all or nearly all of them, but no trace of their origin could be discovered. We have therefore every reason for believing Legg's confession. He could have no possible object in lying to his confidential chum. Besides the whole details that he gives confirms the known facts of the cases, and in many instances, the details given by him, hitherto unknown to me, have been traced and found to be true. Now if these are the things that he boasts of, the question now agitating us is, how many more places has he fired which he has not confessed?

His parents and connections are very respectable. His father was formerly employed in the post office but has been blind for several years past. Both boys have had a fair education. James has worked as clerk in various north end grocery stores for some years. Sam was learning the harness business with Maryin on Argyle street. James is 20 and Sam 18 years of age.

(The Halifax Morning Herald, 23 October 1884)

Halifax was finally rid of these roughs. Jimmy was sentenced to the penitentiary for four years, his brother three years, both convictions for the offence of robbery. Out of respect and concern for their aged parents the charge of arson was not pressed by the Crown.

Jimmy and his brother were not the only members of the "underclass" whom Haligonians sought to expunge, with the assistance of Detective Power. Mollie Donnelly, a professional burglar and prostitute, and native of Galway, Ireland, received a three-year sentence for stealing from the residence of her employer, Mrs. G. Darley Bentley. This, however, was not Mollie's only involvement in the world of Maritime urban crime:

Mollie is a rather prepossessing looking woman of thirty years of age. She came here two years ago, an immigrant passenger on one of the Allan boats bound for Baltimore. Her first exploit was to get drunk, and was taken care of by the police, and as a consequence the steamer went away and left her. For a while she lodged with the janitor of our palatial police station, swept out the city offices, and robbed the unsuspecting and innocent janitor right and left. She was missed by the police but at last turned up in respectable service. In the early part of the summer a series of daring burglaries was committed in the month and within three weeks. Day after day reports were made to the city marshal that houses had been broken into and robbed. The entrances were invariably affected by the basement, and meat, clothing, etc. stolen. The police authorities believed they had another "Quinn" case [another notorious youthful burglar with a history of encounters with the Halifax police] on hand, and started on the hunt for a couple of professional burglars — fellows six feet high, and built proportionately.

Night after night, in all weathers, Detective Power and Sergt. Meagher patrolled and lay around the south end looking for the skilled professional perpetrators of these daring burglaries. But they did not succeed. Among others whose houses were burglarized and robbed were the following: James Richardson, Robie Street; Mrs. McKay, Robie Street; Robert Brown, South Street; K. Gilpin, Carlton Street; William Gilmore, Tower Road; D.H. Burbidge, Robie Street.

Mollie Donnelly meanwhile was a domestic in the family of W.D. Bentley. Mrs. Bentley missed some wearing apparel and made known her loss to the servants. Mollie disappeared a few days later. A day or two afterward, Bentley's house was burglarized at night, one of Mrs. Bentley's trunks ransacked and wearing apparel stolen. Mollie had been keeping company with a soldier, and frequented a house near the Wellington barracks. She used to visit that house very respectably dressed, and leave it in ordinary every day apparel. This fact began to raise suspicion. Finally Mollie was arrested on the charge of stealing from Mrs. Bentley, and from the goods then found in her possession and the facts elicited by the police authorities, it was discovered that Mollie Donnelly had committed all the burglaries recorded in this paragraph. She was a professional female burglar, an experienced, daring, and skilful operator, and the only professional female burglar ever before known in Halifax. All the goods stolen from these houses were disposed of and converted into cash, or stored away for future use. All the people robbed declined to prosecute, except Bentley, and on that charge she only got three years. Had she been prosecuted for all the crimes of which the police could have proven her guilty, she would probably have been awarded thirty years. Her present sentence, therefore, instead of being severe, is an extraordinarily lenient one for her crimes.

(*The Halifax Morning Herald,* 25 October 1884)

THE SABEANS GANG OF ANNAPOLIS VALLEY

Thieves, robbers and con-men did not neglect the rural parts of Nova Scotia. None were perhaps as colorful as Frank Sabeans, who plagued the stores of Annapolis County and of the western part of Kings County at the turn of the century. His alleged exploits were magnified as the respectable sought to control this "outlaw":

News came from the haunts of Frank Sabeans that he is still prowling about seeking what he can devour when hungry and, in order to break the monotony, do a little shop breaking.

John Turner, of West Northfield came to town breathless on Thursday morning with the news that his store had been broken into and goods estimated to be valued $250 stolen. He says he is certain that Sabeans committed the depredation. Yesterday morning Mr. Turner was in town and stated that Sabeans was seen near his place within a day or two. He says this outlaw is harbored by many friends throughout the country and is sometimes driven from place to place. His facility for eluding the constables is great and he still defies arrest. A gentleman in Bridgewater says he saw a man such as Sabeans is described to be in town one night last week.

There are lots of Sabeans yarns and some must be taken with a grain of salt.

A sensation was created last Friday morning when it became known that the store of John E. Hills was broken into and a quantity of valuable coins and goods were stolen. The thief entered by a false key and when he left all that could be noticed to indicate his presence were a few clods of mud and a depleted showcase.

Mr. Hills' gold and silver coins were in the house or they would have shared the fate of the copper ones.

Waterman's store was tried but was too securely fastened to admit of intrusion.

A man whom James Morse declared resembled Sabeans went into Oxner & Duff's store, East Bridgewater last evening, got a drink of water and went up the railway track.

$100 reward has been offered — $50 from the Acadia Pulp Co., and $50 from the Municipality. This ought to be an incentive to the officers of the law to effect Sabeans' capture.

Punishment should also be meted out to those who harbour this outlaw.

(*The Bridgewater Bulletin*, 25 July 1899)

A variety of burglaries in the immediate region were attributed to Sabeans, correctly or incorrectly. One report that he had been shot and followed by a trail of blood brought shouts of exultation. Publication of a letter that he supposedly wrote from Pleasant River only added to the excitement and feeling that his activities were beyond the control of the law:

> ... I intend to make a raid on a few stores this month yet, and next month I intend to make the devil dance in all the province. I have now with me three experts, and will have an old Boston stager next month. I am not afraid to tell the people my ideas as I know they have not a detective in the province to get me although I walked a few feet behind one a week ago at Halifax while my friends rode in the car past me. He was too slow to stop quick ....

(The Bridgewater Bulletin, 15 August 1899)

Periodic sightings of Sabeans in subsequent months without resulting in his apprehension heightened the drama. The manner in which authorities sought to capture him did not escape criticism:

> The detective from Halifax, who went to Annapolis county in search of Frank Sabeans and gang, which has been terrorizing that county and the western part of Kings, has been obliged to return to the city with an empty cage. This is the only instance of the present time that we are aware of that any great effort has been made to bring the gang to justice but this has ended in failure. We dare say that the police of that place are on the lookout but it seems that they are not overexerting themselves in the matter. If they are not sufficiently active let the proper authorities call on the Attorney General for assistance. This has not been done to our knowledge and this thieving party is still at large. Before assistance is asked for, all information that is known in regards to their haunts should be collected. Without this information it would be useless to send an expert to work without any tangible clues. When assistance is called for let the local constables cooperate with the expert detective and have this gang brought to justice and the sooner it is done the

better. Constable Wright was sent to Annapolis to search for parties committing robberies and in his report to Attorney General Longley he said he could not find any clue of them. We could not think he would expect to find them when it came out in city papers the day before that he intended leaving to hunt up Sabeans. By this it would show that the "secret service" of the province was operated on a wonderful scale? Before he was on the scene of action in all probability the gang had either read or heard that they were being sought after and hid themselves. When the officer or officers starts out again we would advise them to keep their movements to themselves and try to see if this gang cannot be caught. The robberies recently committed are now under consideration and no pains will be spared to remedy this nuisance.

(The Kentville Advertiser, 31 May 1901)

Whether the Sabeans "nuisance" continued or not is unclear. Yet his disappearance into history was only temporary. Nine years later we find him charged in Kings County with breaking and entering the store of R.S. Thorne "and stealing therefrom a quantity of goods, also with having in his possession said goods knowing them to have been stolen" *(Kings County Court Book,* 1910. Public Archives of Nova Scotia). Sabeans, ironically, pleaded not guilty. His good fortune continued; he was discharged from custody. No more was heard from the "outlaw."